D1415188

Can You Really Know Your
Future?

Robert Lindsted, Ph.D.

Dedication
This book and its message are dedicated to:

The Glory of God! How wonderful to know that the best thing in life is free! The grace of God and the love of our Lord Jesus compel me to encourage all I meet to turn to Christ. Psalm 115:1 says, "*Not unto us, O Lord, not unto us, but unto thy name give glory, for thy mercy, and for thy truth's sake.*"

My family--my wife, Sharon, and our three children, Pam, Byron, and Kyle. May each of you use your life and all you have to bring glory to our soon coming Lord. May our home be one that truly loves the appearing of Jesus Christ.

Bible Truth Staff: Thanks to Cynthia Weesner, Pat Mueller, Keith Trevolt, Joy Smith, and Mary Beth Williams. Your dedication to the Lord and willingness to carry out every job is an encouragement to me and an honor to Jesus Christ.

Milk and Honey Ministries: Gail Baxter, Deanna Clemence, and the team serving in Yaroslavl, Russia. May God encourage each of you for your interest and sacrifice to bring the gospel to the people of Russia, as well as the rest of the world.

Southwest Radio Church: To all my dear friends at Southwest Radio Church for their encouragement to continually tell forth the good news of the soon return of Christ. Continue the battle, for the coming of the Lord draws near. A special thanks to Buddy Harvey, Stewart Crosley, Christi Killian, Don Glover, and Noah Hutchings.

Chapters 1, 4, 5, and 6 have been taken from *The Next Move, Current Events In Bible Prophecy*, by Robert Lindsted, Ph.D. Chapter 3 has been taken from *Storming Toward Armageddon*, New Leaf Press. Both are available from Bible Truth.

Table of Contents

Why We Believe In Bible Prophecy

I'd like to tell you a story about some hunters. I don't know if you like to hunt or not, but if you do, you may have seen this type of situation before. Along the road by one particular farm there were signs which said, "No Hunting! No Trespassing! Keep Out!" Now every year a group of hunters who always went up and down this same road said, "Isn't it amazing that the biggest and best birds fly right onto that particular farmer's land?" The farmer had a reputation for being the crankiest man in the whole county. Every year when the hunters came, this pattern would be repeated with the best birds flying right onto this farmer's land. One year the hunters decided it couldn't hurt to ask permission to hunt on the farmer's land despite all the signs, so they pulled their car up to his farmyard. They drew straws, and the fellow with the shortest straw had to go knock on the door. "What do you want?" yelled the farmer when the first knock came. The hunter who had drawn the shortest straw thought to himself, "Boy! He really is just as crabby as everyone says he is." Nevertheless, he began to explain to the farmer how every hunting season he and his friends would go by the farm and watch the biggest and best birds take shelter there. Then he asked the farmer if just this once he and his friends could hunt on the land. To the hunter's surprise, that old cranky farmer said, "All right, I'll let you, but only under one condition. Out in the farmyard I have an old horse and that old horse needs to be shot. If you'll shoot that horse, I'll let you hunt." On the way back to the car the hunter thought, "I'll get even with my buddies who gave me the shortest straw." When he got back to the car, the other hunters all asked, "What did he say?" The hunter said, "Boy, that guy made me mad! He made me so mad that I'm going to shoot his horse!" He grabbed his gun and shot the horse. One of the other hunters immediately jumped out of the car, aimed his gun and said, "That makes me so mad that I'm going to shoot his cow!"

Now the reason I'm telling you this story is not to get you to shoot a cow, but to encourage you to react to what you do hear concerning Bible prophecy. I believe God has given us the Bible so we might change our lives to live in agreement with its message. The real purpose of this book is not to provide more facts but to encourage changed lives.

On the night before he retired as a broadcaster, Walter Cronkite remarked how Americans are a people who know more facts than any other people. But even though we have received more information than any other people in all the world, do we live any differently? My prayer is that we may live differently as a result of looking at current events in the light of Bible prophecy.

Why Should We Believe In Bible Prophecy?

To begin with, let's first consider why anyone should believe in Bible prophecy. 2 Peter 1:19-21 is a powerful statement with respect to this question. *"We have also a more sure word of prophecy; whereunto ye do well that ye take heed, as unto a light that shineth in a dark place, until the day dawn, and the day star arise in your hearts: Knowing this first, that no prophecy of the scripture is of any private interpretation. For the prophecy came not in old time by the will of man: but holy men of God spake as they were moved by the Holy Ghost."*

Prophecy is a risky business because prophecy means to predict. It doesn't really matter what area of interest you have, predicting the future is a risky business. Ask the TV weathermen. Even with all the color radar, charts, schooling, and forecasting, if you ask the meteorologists what the weather is going to be tomorrow, they will say, "Well, there's a 40 percent chance of this and a 60 percent chance of that." They're not any better at forecasting than we are, they are just more clever in how they communicate their information.

Have you ever tried to make predictions with regard to politics? Who is going to win the next election? Who is going to be the president four years from now? We can make lots of guesses, but predicting the next election is risky business. The amazing thing about the Bible and Bible prophecy is that there is no guess work. The Bible states history ahead of time. The Bible can tell us all about world powers before they exist. The Bible can let us know things that will happen prior to their happening, and we can be sure these events will be fulfilled exactly as the Bible says. We live in a day and time when much attention has been given to a few people who make predictions. Jeanne Dixon is right less than 10 percent of the time with her predictions, yet all they have to do is put on the front of *The National Enquirer* that "Jeanne Dixon predicts for the 1990s," and people will buy it. People only remember the one or two things that she gets right and forget the 90 percent she misses.

But God's Word is a sure word of prophecy. If you really want to base your life on something sure and solid, base it on the written Word of God. The Bible is God's written record. It contains a sure word of prophecy. "*For the prophecy came not in old time by the will of man: but holy men of God spake* [or wrote] *as they were moved by the Holy Ghost*" (2 Pet. 1:21).

Literally, this passage means that every day as we see current events around us, we become more sure that the Bible is true. Let me ask you this: are you really counting on chapter and verse of this Book for eternal life? I would not stake my life and my eternal future on anything less than the promise of a book that is a "sure word." It would be too risky. Thank God for the written, sure word that He has given in the Bible.

One of the things that makes Christianity unique from every world religion is prophecy. Think about it! The Hindus don't have it. Buddhists don't have it. Christianity is unique in at least two respects: the first is resurrection, the second is prophecy.

At the time of its writing, one-fifth of the Bible was prophetic. If all of this prophecy were put together, it would make up approximately 13 of the 66 books of the Bible. This is equivalent to about one-half of all the New Testament. Now you see how important prophecy is in the Bible.

Why would God give us prophecy? Because prophecy is one of the best proofs that the Bible is true and that it was written by God, not man. No man can predict things like the Bible predicts. For example, in the book of Daniel, the Bible predicts every world power from Daniel's day until now. God names every world power, as well as putting them in order and accurately describing them. The Bible even gives the names of certain kings 175 years before they were born and tells how they will win battles (see Isa. 44:28-45:4). God has given us Bible prophecy to show His Word to be unique, true, and worthy of trust.

God's Word Is Incredible!

As we continue, we will see how truly incredible Bible

prophecy really is. Let's think again about our example of predicting who will be president four years from today. To predict, or to guess the president four years from now, we could list several likely people. But what about trying to name the president twenty years from now, or 100 years from now? You say, "Don't be ridiculous! That person hasn't been born yet." But the Bible gave the name of a specific king, told of the battle, and how the battle would be won 175 years before the king was ever born. Do you see the difference between a guess and Bible prophecy? This same God who gave man these prophecies controls current events, and I believe that more Bible prophecy has been fulfilled in the last five years than in the entire history of man. I really believe the Bible is the guide to the future. Without this Book we have no light on the plan of God for today or tomorrow.

One of the best ways to develop confidence in Bible prophecy is to look at some specific prophecies that have been fulfilled in the past. A math professor by the name of Dr. Peter Stoner did such a study on fulfilled prophecy. Dr Stoner looked at only 11 fulfilled prophecies concerning the first coming of Christ. These were well known prophecies such as: the prophet Micah, 700 B.C., saying that Christ would be born in Bethlehem; the prophet Malachi, 400 B.C., saying that Christ would have a forerunner; and Zechariah, 800 years before Christ was born, saying that Christ would enter into Jerusalem on a colt, the foal of an ass. Zechariah also prophesied that Christ would be betrayed by a friend, would be sold for 30 pieces of silver, and the money would then be used to buy a potter's field. The Old Testament says that Christ would be silent at His trial. The Bible also says, in the book of Psalms, that they would gamble for His clothing. Dr. Stoner chose 11 such prophecies.

According to Dr. Stoner, if you were to take only the

chosen 11 prophecies, the odds of them coming true would be one out of 1,000,000,000,000,000,000,000,000,000,000. (If you like big numbers, this is called a octillion.) In other words, you would have a better chance of making a box with a volume of 80 cubic miles, filling it with dimes, marking one dime, and then having a blindfolded person pick the marked dime on the first try! Remember, these are the odds for only 11 of the prophecies which Christ fulfilled. But as you come to the Bible you must realize that Christ did not fulfill only 11 prophecies. At least 27 prophecies were fulfilled by Christ on one day! There are literally hundreds of prophecies in the Bible. Someone has counted 333 prophecies which relate just to Christ's coming. More precisely, 109 of these prophecies describe details concerning His first coming. These are prophecies which tell how He would come as a baby, would be crucified, and would come alive again at resurrection. With these 109 prophetic details, what is the chance of them all being fulfilled by chance? Either these prophetic details were fulfilled by accident, or the Bible is indeed the written Word of God. Now you can see why I don't believe this Book is an accident.

To go a little further with this thought, what if we were to arbitrarily say that the odds of any one of these 109 prophecies coming true was 50-50? Of course, you realize that this is ridiculous, and the odds really are not 50-50. That would be like saying there were only two cities in the world and by accident Christ was born in Bethlehem. As a matter of fact, there were over 1,000 cities at the time of Christ's birth. So really the odds would be at least one out of 1,000.

If the odds were just 50-50, that would be the same as flipping a coin to get "heads." To fulfill 109 prophecies by accident would be like flipping 109 "heads" in a row. To show you how incredible it would be to count on flipping 109 "heads" in a row, or to believe that 109 prophecies came true by accident, consider this. We would need two people to flip a quarter one time to be assured of getting one "head." The odds say one person should get a "head" and the other a "tail." So it takes two people flipping a coin one time to get one "head" by chance. But Christ did not fulfill only one prophecy!

What about the odds of fulfilling two prophecies by accident? Now you need four people, each flipping a quarter. Two of the people get "heads" and the other two get "tails." The two who get "heads" now flip again, and the odds say one would get a "head" and the other a "tail." In other words, it takes four people flipping a quarter two times in order to get two "heads" in a row.

The number of people required grows exponentially as the number of "heads" in a row increases. For example, three "heads" in a row with 50-50 odds would require eight people flipping a coin three times. In order to get ten "heads" in a row, 1,024 people would be required to flip a coin ten times to achieve a streak of ten "heads." But Christ didn't fulfill only ten prophecies!

To build a model to show 20 "accidents" in a row, we need 1,048,576 people. They would flip their quarters 20 times each and only one person would get 20 "heads" in a row. What about 40 "accidents" in a row? Here is what we need to do. Imagine 200 planet earths. Put 5 billion people, each with a quarter, on each of the planets. Only one person out of all 5 billion people on all 200 planets would get 40 "heads" in a row. Is it even reasonable to believe that Christ fulfilled 40 prophecies by accident? But Christ didn't fulfill only 40 prophecies.

What would be the odds of Christ fulfilling 109 prophecies by accident? NASA now says there are 100 billion galaxies. The Milky Way, our galaxy, is only one small galaxy. These galaxies average 100 billion stars per galaxy. If we could put 5 billion people on each of these 100 billion stars in each of the 100 billion galaxies, and give each person a quarter, the odds say no one would get 100 "heads" in a row! This is why I believe Christ is a fulfillment of Bible prophecy. When Jesus Christ came He fulfilled 109 very specific prophecies. Prophecy is God writing a sure word, not just the guesses of men.

In these last days in a very special and direct way, God is fulfilling His Word so that you and I might realize that Christ not only came the first time, but He is coming again. For every one detail God gave about Christ's first coming, there are two prophecies concerning His second coming. If Christ does not come the second time, this would make God twice as big a liar than if Christ had not come the first time. Be assured, Christ will come again! The promises of God are guaranteed!

2 Corinthians 1:20 establishes the fact that God is in the business of making promises. Actually, Bible prophecies are the promises of God. 2 Corinthians 1:20 says: "*For all the promises of God in him are yea, and in him Amen, unto the glory of God by us.*" How wonderful to have a God that not only makes promises, but is able to fulfill them!

Several years ago when my children were growing up and I was on the road a lot, I told my son, Byron, he could pick any activity for us to do together on the coming Saturday. Byron said, "Okay, Dad, let's go to the zoo." To be honest I wasn't very excited about going to the zoo. There were a lot of other things I would like to have done, but since I made a promise to my boy, I said, "All right, we'll go to the zoo on Saturday." Now being a child and believing that every promise made by a parent will come true, he could hardly wait for Saturday. Monday came and he said, "Dad, is this Saturday?" I said, "No, not yet." Then Tuesday came and he said, "Dad, is this Saturday?" I said, "No." Then Friday came and I said, "Byron, tomorrow is Saturday." So Saturday morning very early, about 6 o'clock, he came into my bedroom, pried open my eyes, and woke me up saying, "Dad, it's Saturday! This is the day you promised to take me to the zoo!" You see, a child believes the promises made by a parent, and we are to believe the promises that God has made, because every promise of God is "Yea and Amen." Often when I make promises, circumstances may arise so that I can't fulfill those promises. But God has veracity! This means He is in such control that He can fulfill His promises. It is wonderful to have a God who not only makes promises, but is able to fulfill each promise He makes!

Look at some of those promises, especially those that are related to the coming of Christ. One of them is John 14:1-3: *"Let not your heart be troubled: ye believe in God, believe also in me. In my Father's house are many mansions: if it were not so, I would have told you. I go to prepare a place for you. And if I go and prepare a place for you, I will come again, and receive you unto myself; that where I am, there ye may be also."*

I believe when Christ says, *"And if I go and prepare a place for you, I will come again,"* that's a promise. It is a promise that Christ made stating He would definitely come again. Did He go? Yes, He did! Is He preparing a place for us? Yes, He is! Will He come again? I believe by the promises of God, which are "Yea and Amen," Christ will indeed come again.

Another promise of God related to the coming of Christ is found in the Gospel of Matthew. In Matthew 24:32-35, Christ, speaking to His disciples, said: *"Now learn a parable of the fig tree; When his branch is yet tender, and putteth forth leaves, ye know that summer is nigh: So likewise ye, when ye shall see all these things, know that it is near, even at the doors. Verily I say unto you, This generation shall not pass, till all these things be fulfilled. Heaven and earth shall pass away, but my words shall not pass away."*

Isn't this a beautiful promise of God? Christ speaks to the disciples concerning a fig tree. I believe the parable of the fig tree that is mentioned here is a picture of the nation of Israel. After Israel became a nation again in May 1948, they adopted a fig tree as one of their symbols. I believe that Israel is also represented in the New Testament by a fig tree in other passages too. Just several days earlier, as recorded in Matthew 21:17-21, Christ was walking with His disciples along the countryside and they came to a fig tree. This fig tree bore no fruit. As Christ spoke, the disciples saw the tree wither up. The disciples were amazed that He dealt so harshly with the tree, but I believe the message is this: Christ had come to Israel, and since there was no spiritual fruit, they were going to be cut off to wither away. You see, Israel rejected Christ, the Messiah, the Savior of the world. They had Him crucified. He went to the cross and He died for their sins, as well as my sins and yours. Because they rejected Christ, they could bear no spiritual fruit. (That would be a spiritual rebirth.) They were then cut off as a nation--and that occurred 37 years later under Titus, a Roman general, as he marched through Jerusalem. (What is described in Matthew 24:32-35 is a political rebirth which I believe was fulfilled in a marvelous way in May 1948.)

God's Exact Timing!

The promises of God often involve a time frame, but sometimes I think we doubt if God is really in such control of all circumstances that will enable Him to bring about the exact fulfillment of His promises. Let's go back in the Bible to find some examples of God making promises with time commitments. We'll see how wonderfully God is able to fulfill each promise precisely as it is written. Let's begin in Genesis 6:3 with a very familiar story: *"And the Lord said, My spirit shall not always strive with man, for that he also is flesh: yet his days shall be an hundred and twenty years."* When God was talking to Noah, He said judgment was going to come because of evil and corruption on the face of the earth, and Noah had 120 years. What a message! What a promise! God promised Noah 120 years.

Some people have said, "Well, that really means that men are going to live to be 120 years old." If that is the meaning of the passage, why do the first dozen people after the ark violate it? It can't mean that. God meant that in exactly 120 years he was going to send judgment.

The story of Noah is a remarkable one! If you stop and imagine how this all came about, it is truly incredible. God came to Noah and said, "Noah, Noah! I want you to build an ark." I can see Noah, who was a righteous man, saying, "All right, I'll do it." He goes over to the Webster's dictionary and looks up "a-r-k," and it says, "Has not been built yet." Remember, at the time God spoke to Noah, it had never rained upon the face of the earth. He said to Noah, "Noah, I'm going to destroy the wickedness that is on the face of the earth by a flood. But, Noah, I want you to build a boat (an ark) and that boat is going to be your safety and your salvation from this flood!" God said that judgment was going to come in 120 years. Now I think the people in Noah's day laughed at him and said, "Noah, I think it's crazy to believe a promise like that. There has never been any rain. Why in the world should you build a boat?" Yet Noah believed the promises of God. Not in 119 years or in 121 years, but in exactly 120 years an overwhelming flood came. Only Noah and those in the ark who believed the promises of God were spared from that judgment. It might have looked unlikely for that promise to be fulfilled, but God promised judgment, and the promise was fulfilled in an exact way, at the exact time. Every promise of God is "yes" and guaranteed.

Then in Genesis 15 we find another promise of God. This time the promise of God is made to a man named Abram. *"And he said unto Abram, Know of a surety that thy seed shall be a stranger in a land that is not their's, and shall serve them; and they shall afflict them four hundred years....But in the fourth generation they shall come hither again: for the iniquity of the Amorites is not yet full"* (Gen. 15:13,16).

This promise of God to Abram also has a time commitment in it, just as our passage in Matthew 24 has a time commitment. After Abram had already been in the land for 30 years, God told him that he and his descendants would be in the land for 400 more years, making a total of 430 years. God also said this time span of 400 more years would take place in the fourth generation.

It is interesting to note that the generations here average 100 years each. There are generations in the Bible which are 30 years, 33 years, 40 years, 70 years, and even 100 years. Therefore, a generation is an unspecified amount of time used by God for maturing and working with a nation or an individual. We cannot say it is exactly 30 years, or 40 years, or 100 years. It can vary, depending on the plan and time of God. In the particular case in Genesis 15, the 430 years was represented by four generations. This is an amazing prediction and promise of God. In 400 years He would deliver Abram's descendants from Egypt.

When God promised to deliver Israel in the 430th year and the fourth generation, there were people who actually believed the promises of God so literally that they thought God would do exactly that--deliver the slave nation of Israel from the powerful Egyptian nation. In this group of people were the parents of Moses. Hebrews 11 tells of their marvelous faith in the promises of God. In verse 23 it says that the parents of Moses hid him because they saw he was a "proper" child. I think those parents thought, "Our son is the fourth generation, and we are coming to the end of the 430 years. Wouldn't it be wonderful if God would use our boy, Moses, to deliver the children of Israel from their bondage?" Thank God for parents who have dreams and plans for their children that are spiritual!

What a story it turns out to be! Exodus 12:41-42 reads: *"And it came to pass at the end of the four hundred and thirty years, even the selfsame day it came to pass, that all the hosts of the Lord went out from the land of Egypt. It is a night to be much observed unto the Lord for bringing them out from the land of Egypt: this is that night of the Lord to be observed of all the children of Israel in their generations."*

Do you see that? God was not even one day late in fulfilling His promise to Abram. It was as God said--after 430 years and four generations He delivered Israel. God's promise came true right on the day!

Another interesting promise of God is found in Numbers 13:21-25. Twelve men are sent to spy out the Promised Land. According to verse 25, they spent 40 days there. But in chapter 14:34, God said they would spend one year wandering in the wilderness for each day they had spent searching the Promised Land. Because they doubted His promise, they would bear their iniquities for 40 years. Notice that in Numbers 14:35 He says, *"I the Lord have said, I will surely do it unto all this evil congregation, that are gathered together against me: in this wilderness they shall be consumed, and there they shall die."* Doesn't that sound like a promise? Does it have a time frame? Did God keep it? He sure did!

Another beautiful promise of God with a time frame is

recorded in Jeremiah 25:9-11. God, through the prophet Jeremiah, said that Babylon would control Israel for 70 years. God makes a promise to be fulfilled in a specific time period.

Now go to the final two verses of Daniel 5. There we read of a feast given by the ruler of Babylon. During the feast Belshazzar, the ruler, sees a hand writing on the wall. He quickly beckons for the wise men, but none could interpret the meaning of the writing. Then he called for Daniel and said, "Daniel, can you read the writing? What is the message? If you can interpret the writing you'll become the third ruler in the kingdom." Daniel said, "I can read it. But since I can read it, I want no part of this kingdom. God has found this kingdom wanting. He has weighed it, and it falls short. Soon it will be cut off!"

How did Daniel know? I believe Daniel knew because he believed the sure Word of God. Daniel 9:2 says Daniel understood the time frame God spoke of in Jeremiah 25:9-11. What a promise and what a fulfillment! That very night the Medes and the Persians overtook Babylon. The end of the 70-year rule of Babylon transpired according to God's schedule. What a God we have! He makes mighty promises, and all His promises are guaranteed!

We could look at a number of other promises with time frames, but maybe you are noticing that all of these promises have been from the Old Testament. Did God make promises in the New Testament? Did those promises have time frames? Was He still able to keep each promise?

Yes, God continued to make promises. Matthew 20:17-19 says, "*And Jesus going up to Jerusalem took the twelve disciples apart in the way, and said unto them, Behold, we go up to Jerusalem; and the Son of man shall be betrayed unto the chief priests and unto the scribes, and they shall condemn him to death, And shall deliver him to the Gentiles to mock, and to scourge, and to crucify him: and the third day he shall rise again."*

Do you see that? This is in the New Testament! As Christ talked to His disciples, He clearly promised them that He would die, and three days later He would rise again. God made a promise and Christ fulfilled that promise, because every promise of God is "yes," and in Him, Christ, guaranteed. Did God make promises for modern times? I believe He did.

Let's return to our passage in Matthew 24. The Lord Jesus Christ tells us to learn the parable of the fig tree. I believe He is speaking specifically of Israel. Christ says you'll see Israel come back as a nation again as represented by a young, tender branch. This branch is a political, national Israel, but not a spiritual or fruit-bearing Israel. I believe the Lord makes this promise: the generation that sees Israel come back shall not pass till all things are fulfilled. Again, we don't know the length of the generation--30 years, 40 years, 70 years, 100 years, or even more--but God's promise is that heaven and earth will pass away but His promise and His words shall not pass away.

Have You Claimed the Promises of God?

The same God who made promises to Noah, to Abram, to Daniel, to the prophet Jeremiah, to His disciples, and fulfilled every one of these promises (even to the exact time), has made some tremendous promises concerning current events. We will look at these in following chapters. God has also given us the greatest promise concerning eternal life. Look at John 3:36: *"He that believeth on the Son hath everlasting life: and he that believeth not the Son shall not see life; but the wrath of God abideth on him."*

You see, this is a promise of God. The same God that has fulfilled all these other promises says that if you will accept by faith what Christ did on the cross, you will have everlasting life. If we will acknowledge that we are sinners and that we have come short of the standard that God has set, receiving the work Christ did as He willingly went to the cross, we will have salvation. On the cross Christ bled and died to pay the debt of man's sin, and on the third day, according to the promise of God, He came alive again. Now God promises that anyone who believes on the Son and receives Christ for who He is (the Lord of lords, the King of kings, the Savior of the world), will be given everlasting life. Anyone who does not believe in the Son shall not see life, but God's promise to such a person is the wrath of God. Have you claimed the promises of God? If not, will you receive Jesus Christ as your personal Savior? A belief in Bible prophecy is a belief in the veracity of God to fulfill promises. My salvation rests on His promise. What are you resting on for your salvation, dear friend? I trust it is the finished work and promises of Christ.

Israel--
The Barren Fig Tree Coming to Life

Often people want to know a time that would indicate we are living in the "last days", a time when many predictions of the Bible are to come true. Signs are not new! Even today, we find that people are curious about signs and fortune tellers, but there is a great difference between those who make predictions and the prophecies of the Bible. The Bible's prophecies *always* come true! As we have already seen, 2 Corinthians 1:20 says:

"For all the promises of God in him are yea, and in him Amen, unto the glory of God by us." Even the people of Jesus' day wanted to see signs. Matthew 16:1-4 records an answer which the Lord gave to the Pharisees and Sadducees when they came asking Him for a sign: *"The Pharisees also with the Sadducees came, and tempting desired him that he would shew them a sign from heaven. He answered and said unto them, When it is evening, ye say, It will be fair weather: for the sky is red. And in the morning, it will be foul weather today: for the sky is red and lowering. O ye hypocrites, ye can discern the face of the sky; but can ye not discern the signs of the times? A wicked and adulterous generation seeketh after a sign; and there shall no sign be given unto it, but the sign of the prophet Jonas. And he left them, and departed."*

What an answer He gave. He reminded them that they

seemed to be more skilled at predictiing the weather than they were able to see what God was doing before their very eyes. Isn't this true today? So many people will make a guess whether the weather will be cold or hot, sunshine or rain, but then they fail to see the important signs concerning where we are with respect to God's prophetic program. The story these verses describe are such that even in the days of Jesus Christ, they predicted the weather by looking at the clouds. Actually, these verses agree with an old navy saying:

> *"Red at night is the sailor's delight,*
> *Red in the morning is a sailor's warning."*

Jesus makes it clear that those who know Him as Lord and Savior will not be looking for signs, but they will be looking for the Lord Himself to come. There is a great difference. Even though the Bible has hundreds of signs, many of which have already been fulfilled, and all of which will soon be fulfilled, they are not signs for the Rapture, the time when Christ will come and take those who have trusted in Him as their personal Savior to be with Him in heaven. Instead, the signs are an indicator that we are approaching the latter days when the Tribulation and the Kingdom of God will take place. The time frame for these events will be discussed more in chapter 4.

But what about signs? Are signs important? Do they have a bearing on today? Yes, Bible signs are very important and that is why God gave so many. We could look at literally hundreds of passages that deal with Bible signs. One sign of great importance is Israel. But remember, these signs indicate what Israel will be like in the latter days! In other words, these are signs for the Tribulation and the Millennial Kingdom. But as we see these times approaching, we know that the coming of Christ for those who trust in Him must be very near.

Israel as a Fig Tree

In Matthew 24:32-35 we have the great sign of the parable of the fig tree: *"Now learn a (the) parable of the fig tree; When his branch is yet tender, and putteth forth leaves, ye know that summer is nigh: So likewise ye, when ye shall see all these things, know that it is near, even at the doors. Verily I say unto you, this generation shall not pass, till all these things be fulfilled. Heaven and earth shall pass away, but my words shall not pass away."* It is interesting to note it is not just a parable about any fig tree, but it states "now learn *the* parable of the fig tree." In other words, He was referring to a specific incident. Also notice in this lesson that the fig tree does not bear fruit, but simply shoots forth leaves and branches. When we see this fig tree sprouting leaves and branches, we know the time Christ is referring to in this setting must be very near. Christ goes on to promise that heaven and earth shall pass away, before even one of His words, or prophecies will not be fulfilled. In other words, this really is a sure promise made by Christ! So what is the setting when Christ spoke this parable?

In Matthew 24:3, the disciples are asking Christ three important questions. No doubt the disciples were excited as they heard Him begin speaking about the coming of the Kingdom of God. They were especially excited because they believed He was the Messiah. They also believed the Messiah would come and set up a kingdom which would overthrow the Roman powers and they would be a free people again! You can't blame them for being excited. And you can't blame them for believing this might be the right time as they heard the Lord Himself speak of the Kingdom of God. They had listened to His messages. They had walked with Him from village to village and knew His character. They had watched His miracles. They were convinced He really was the Messiah.

As well, they were familiar with the Old Testament, where in Zechariah 14, it states that the Messiah would come to the Mount of Olives, and when He stands there, He would split the mountain in two. They were no doubt familiar with the many passages which declare when the Messiah comes He would rule from the Temple. As they looked across from the Mount of Olives, they could see Herod's temple glistening in the sun. All around the top of Herod's temple was a band of pure gold. As the sun would rise in the morning and peak over the Mount of Olives, the first rays from the sun hit the gold band around Herod's dome, lighting the sky with a golden hue. Jerusalem was such a spectacular sight with the sun coming up, that historians would often say if you have not seen the Temple, you have not seen beauty. I'm sure the disciples could only imagine Christ ruling and reigning from this Temple.

Matthew 24:2 indicates that Christ answered their requests concerning the Temple by saying, "The temple you think would be so great to rule from will not be left standing. Before things are done, there will not be a stone left upon another which will not be thrown down." No doubt the disciples could not believe what they were hearing! If He was preaching about the Kingdom and He was the Messiah, then why would He refuse to use this Temple? Would it really be destroyed? This is exactly what prompts the three questions found in Matthew 24:3. First, the disciples asked the Lord, "*When* shall these things be?" Next, they asked, "*What* will be the sign of thy coming?" Thirdly, they asked, "*What* will be the sign of the end of the age?"

The entire chapter of Matthew 24 is really a Tribulation text. The signs given there indicate what the conditions will be during the the seven years of Tribulation on the earth. It will be a dreadful time when God's judgments will be poured out on those who have refused to receive Christ as their personal Savior. Again, we will discuss much of these events in our later chapters, but our intent here is to look at the signs. It is during the midst of this discussion of signs, that Christ gives the important lesson concerning the parable of the fig tree.

It is important for us, however, to realize that Christ really did know what was taking place. For remember, within a short time, Christ would be taken and become the subject of a mock trial. The conclusions of this mock trial would be for Him to go to a cross and die. But after He was buried, three days later, He would rise again! It is amazing that even these events were predicted in the Old Testament in great detail. Already we have pointed out in chapter one how it would be impossible for them to be fulfilled by accident. These events were designed by God Himself! Acts 1:6 records that after Christ's crucifixion and resurrection, the disciples again asked Him if this might be the right time for Him to set up His Kingdom. Can you see they were still excited about this possibility? Again, I don't think we can blame them for such enthusiasm. But notice what it says in Acts 1:6-7: *"When they therefore were come together, they asked of him, saying, Lord, wilt thou at this time restore again the kingdom to Israel? And he said unto them, It is not for you to know the times or the seasons, which the Father hath put in his own power."*

Notice also from verse 12 they were again on the Mount of Olives. In other words they were saying, "We still believe you are the Messiah. We still believe this is the right place. Is this going to be the time when You will fulfill all the promises and set up a Kingdom?" However, verse 7 clearly indicates that it would not be in the disciples' life when such a kingdom would be set up. Yes, the Bible does promise He will come and rule and reign.

Luke 1:30-33 says: *"And the angel said unto her, Fear not, Mary: for thou hast found favour with God. And, behold, thou shalt conceive in thy womb, and bring forth a son, and shalt call his name JESUS. He shall be great, and shall be called the Son of the Highest: and the Lord God shall give unto him the throne of his father David: And he shall reign over the house of Jacob for ever; and of his kingdom there shall be no end."* The first part of this great prophecy indicates the Messiah would come being born of a virgin. This was also predicted by the prophet in Isaiah 7:14. It not only predicts Mary would have a virgin-born child, but the child would be a son! Then it predicts the child's name would be Jesus! All of these came true. We celebrate it at Christmas.

However, the prediction goes on. It says before He is done, Christ will be great and He will rule on the throne of David. At Jesus' first coming, He didn't rule one day on the throne of David, nor did He rule over the house of Jacob or Israel. Yet these are promises made in the Bible. This is why we know He must come again. When He comes again, He *will* set up a Kingdom and He *will* rule and reign. Once He begins to rule and reign, there will be no end to His kingdom. These promises are stated clearly in God's Word. But, of course, the disciples did not have the advantage of the past 2,000 years to look back over history and fulfilled prophecies. They were still looking for Christ to set up His Kingdom immediately upon His resurrection.

Thirty-eight years later, in A.D. 70, the Romans would tighten their grip on Jerusalem. Eventually they would not only destroy the city, but they would burn the Temple. As the Temple, in all of its beauty burned, with the flames melting the golden band around the top of Herod's Temple, the soldiers made a plan. Their plan was to tear the Temple apart brick by brick and stone by stone to retrieve the gold which had now melted and dripped down every stone and every brick! The words of Christ in Matthew 24:2 were literally fulfilled. Yes, the promise was fulfilled 38 years after Christ made it, but it was fulfilled exactly as He said! This is one way Jesus Christ proves that He is God. For only God can know the future in such detail. As well, only God can control the future. If He didn't know or control the future, He would not be God. But the fulfilled prophecy of the Bible proved Jesus Christ is who He claims to be, the Messiah, the Savior of mankind, God incarnate.

So Matthew 24:32-35 gives a great sign. Jesus says when you see the fig tree coming forth, you will know this is the time My coming again to set up a Kingdom will be near. I personally believe the generation He is speaking of in Matthew 24:34, implies the generation which witnesses the fig tree beginning to shoot forth leaves and branches. This generation would then be the very people who would see these leaves and branches coming on the fig tree. Christ's predictions concerning His ruling and reigning will be fulfilled. What does this fig tree represent, and is this fig tree still important for us today? These are important questions as we study God's promises and prophecies in the Bible.

Again, to clearly understand what Christ is referring to in Matthew 24, it is important to refer to the story of Matthew 21:18-22. On this occasion, Christ was walking through a city and saw a fig tree along the way which had no fruit. Because it had no fruit, Christ spoke sharp words to the fig tree. It withered up and became a barren tree. It was quite a lesson for the disciples. They were amazed at Christ's power. However, the real meaning of this recorded incident is only understood as we read the parable in Matthew 24:32-

35. I believe Christ is saying when you see this once- withered fig tree coming to life again, then you will know this is the very time as predicted in the Scripture. The time they were asking about is when the end of the age would be. They were asking about when He would come to set up His Kingdom. They were asking about the signs indicating they were living in those days.

I believe this fig tree picture is Israel. Because Israel rejected the ministry of Christ when He came the first time, I believe they were cut off from the promises of God. Israel as a nation became a barren fig tree from A.D. 70 all the way until 1948. For 1,878 years, there was no nation of Israel, no land to really call their own. However, Jesus Christ was promising there would be a time when this fig tree which was withered up, would once again bear leaves and branches. The rebirth of this fig tree, I believe, was the rebirth of the nation of Israel, as fulfilled on May 14, 1948.

The fig tree is often referred to in the Old Testament and many people believe some of these references directly apply to the nation of Israel. But the real proof Israel is compared to a fig tree, may best be seen from another parable found in Luke 13:6-9: *"He spake also this parable; A certain man had a fig tree planted in his vineyard; and he came and sought fruit thereon, and found none. Then said he unto the dresser of his vineyard, Behold, these three years I come seeking fruit on this fig tree, and find none: cut it down; why cumbereth it the ground? And he answering said unto him, Lord, let it alone this year also, till I shall dig about it, and dung it: And if it bear fruit, well: and if not, then after that thou shalt cut it down."*

This parable refers to a man who had a special tree--a fig tree. He planted it in a special place--a vineyard. It was planted for a special purpose--to bear figs. At the end of three years when there was no fruit on this fig tree, the command was given to cut it down! However, the decision was made to let the fig tree stand one more year and if it didn't bear fruit, then go ahead and remove it.

What a picture this is of the nation of Israel. For three years Christ came doing incredible miracles, speaking magnificent messages and living in such a way as He blessed every one He came into contact with. However, as a whole, the nation of Israel did not receive Him. The Bible even predicts in John 1:11 that He would come unto His own and His own would receive Him not.

Notice the request that the fig tree remain one more year. It would be during this extension that the nation of Israel would see Jesus Christ die on the cross, be buried and rise again. They would see Him fulfill all 109 predictions and prophecies concerning His first coming. If they did not respond to the fulfillment of the ancient prophets about Christ's first coming, then there would be devastation on the nation of Israel. This occurred in A.D. 70. What a tragedy for the fig tree to be withered up, but what a hope that there would be yet another day when this same tree would begin to bear leaves and branches. I believe the barren fig tree which comes to life is none other than Israel. In other words, Israel is a sign of when the Tribulation is coming, after which Christ will come to set up His Kingdom on the earth. Before these events ever take place, Christ will come for those who have placed their trust in Him.

This is a good time for each of us to examine, "Have we really received Christ as our personal Savior?" This is not being religious and it is not just trying to do good works. Rather, it is acknowledging the Bible condemns all of us as sinners by our nature and by our practice. It also means acknowledging that salvation can only come when we recognize Jesus Christ died on the cross for each one of us personally. Since Christ had no sin of His own, His death on the cross was payment for our sins. The Bible states in Romans 6:23: *"For the wages of sin is death; but the gift of God is eternal life through Jesus Christ our Lord."*

With Christ's death He was paying the debt I owe...and you owe. Now, when we receive Christ as our personal Savior, His death is payment for our sin. We can be forgiven by God. We can be saved and on our way to heaven.

Old Testament Prophecies Concerning Israel

The sign of Israel as an indicator of the last days is not restricted to just these passages in the gospels. There are literally dozens of prophecies in the Old Testament concerning Israel as a great sign of the end time. These prophecies are extremely interesting and valuable as we study the predictions made concerning Israel in the last days.

Signs Given to the Prophet Ezekiel

Some 2,600 years ago, God spoke to the prophet Ezekiel. Essentially, He was telling Ezekiel *when* the last days would be. The last days would be a time when God would fulfill all of His promises to Israel. It would also be the time when Christ would come to rule and reign. The description of some of these signs are found beginning in Ezekiel 36:19,24: *"And I scattered them among the heathen, and they were dispersed through the countries: according to their way and according to their doings I judged them....For I will take you from among the heathen, and gather you out of all countries, and will bring you into your own land."*

Notice what God says. He says you will know the time of the last days because the nation of Israel will be scattered among many nations, and then He will gather them right back into their own land. In reality, we have observed this actually happen! Remember that in A.D. 70, after the Romans destroyed Jerusalem, the Jewish people were scattered to the four corners of the earth. Only since 1948 have we really seen the Jewish people regathered into their own land. It is an even greater miracle when you consider that most people, when they were taken captive by another nation for even several hundred years, normally adopted that nation's religion, languages, and customs. But after over 1,800 years out of their own land, the Jews have come back with the same language, the same customs, and the same religion. Surely this is a great fulfillment of what was promised by God to the prophet Ezekiel in Ezekiel 36:24.

Isaiah also speaks of the regathering of Israel. Isaiah 43:5-6 says: *"Fear not: for I am with thee: I will bring thy seed from the east, and gather thee from the west; I will say to the north, Give up; and to the south, Keep not back: bring my sons from far, and my daughters from the ends of the earth."* Notice the prophet said they would regather from the east, the west, the south, and the north. Several years ago I was talking to a military leader in Israel. He indicated it was clear we must be living in the last days. When I questioned him why he felt so strongly about it, he referred to this passage. He said, "It is interesting to note that the very first group of people who returned to the land of Israel after becoming a nation in 1948, were from China, out of the east. The next group to repopulate the land of Israel were from the west, out of Europe. We have been watching Russian Jews leave Russia, out of the north, and come back to settle in Israel. Finally, several years ago, we watched what was called 'Operation Moses.' Ethiopian Jews were airlifted out of Ethiopia and brought to settle in Israel, out of the south." To this Jewish man, it was clear we were watching the fulfillment of Israel being regathered as promised by God through the ancient prophet Isaiah.

As we look at Israel, regathered in the land after being scattered, I believe we do see a great sign and fulfillment of God's Word. Some might say, "Couldn't this have been fulfilled by Israel returning after Babylon or one of the other captivities?" The reason why I can say it wasn't fulfilled by the return from Babylon, is because Christ Himself, in Luke 21:24 says: *"And they shall fall by the edge of the sword, and shall be led away captive into all nations: and Jerusalem shall be trodden down of the Gentiles, until the times of the Gentiles be fulfilled."* In other words, Christ repeats this same promise again. He says there would be a time the Jews would be led away captive. There would be a time when Jerusalem would be under the control of Gentile world powers. But there would also be a time when the Jews would regather in their land, and Jerusalem would be under the control of Jewish people. Since Christ speaks of this in the future, we know it was not fulfilled by past powers during the Old Testament times before the days of Christ. Since He was speaking of the future, we know it must be after those words were spoken in A.D. 30. What grander fulfillment than when Israel became a nation in 1948! As well, it is interesting to realize that after the 1967 war, Israel again gained control of the city of Jerusalem. We must conclude God's Word did predict the future! What a thrill to see God give signs concerning Israel and to have them fulfilled.

There is another great sign mentioned by God to the prophet Ezekiel in chapter 36. Beginning in verses 26-35, God tells the prophet Ezekiel there would be another way he will be able to clearly recognize when the last days are occuring, that is when Israel is once again reestablished as a barren fig tree coming to life. He mentions He will put a new heart in them, a heart of flesh and not of stone. He also mentions He will increase the productivity of the land. Verse 35 expresses it best: *"And they shall say, This land that was desolate is become like the garden of Eden; and the waste and desolate and ruined cities are become fenced, and are inhabited."* Surely this would be a sign easy to recognize. It says when the deserts of Israel become like the Garden of Eden, then we will know we are living in those days when God is fulfilling His promise and prophecies concerning Israel in the last days. Is this occurring today?

We can verify the fulfillment of this prophecy by looking at a very interesting article published in *The Saturday Evening Post* in September 1987, pages 48-49. The title of the article is "Israel's Miracle Food From the Desert." It has a subtitle which reveals an amazing fact: *"From sand and a little bit of salty water, the farms of the Negev Desert are feeding themselves and much of Europe."* The article expresses the idea that at one time the Negev Desert was once pronounced "uninhabitable". But now it has become the home of over a half-million people. In addition, the very area which was once a desert, is now a lush farmland. This includes 250 new, thriving farm communities.

This article goes on to state another amazing fact: that Israel is now growing special crops in the desert. These crops are the result of Israel planting "desert designer crops" in the sand and watering them with brackish water. The brackish water contains a concentration of salt 20 times that of normal drinking water! Not only is it incredible to see crops growing in the desert using salt water, but the yields are also spectacular. The article quotes a farmer, who three times a year is getting high yields of melons, tomatoes, eggplants, peppers, dates, zucchinis and avocados. These crops are then shipped to markets in Europe weeks or months before the local produce arrives. This particular farmer is growing about 60 tons of food per acre--that is four to six times what an average farmer would grow on a yearly basis. As I read this article, I couldn't help but believe we are looking at a great fulfillment of Bible prophecy.

People in the United States were so struck with this idea of raising crops in the desert, that *The New York Times*, June 19, 1990, page B-6, records an exciting article. It tells about people wanting to grow crops in the deserts of the United States. Unfortunately, the success was not as good as in Israel. The suggestion was made to use salt water! Again, it was simply copying the process used in Israel. But unfortunately, the results of this did not prove the same productivity of Israel.

Another article out of *Spotlight on Israel*, October 1988, page 13, speaks of Israel producing out of season fruit such as peaches, plums, apricots, nectarines and cherries. These fruits are selling for up to ten times the normal in-season price on European markets! The article reports that Israel is now exporting flowers too. It is hard to believe the countries they are selling flowers to include Germany, England, France, and even Holland!

The Bible further predicted Israel would be a source of fruit and vegetation in the last days, as found in Isaiah 27:6: *"He shall cause them that come of Jacob to take root: Israel shall blossom and bud, and fill the face of the world with fruit."*

To make the prediction that someday Israel would bud, blossom, and fill the face of the world with fruit, was an incredible prediction. But today, we are watching the small area of Israel become known as the "breadbasket" of the world. I remember several years ago flying through Europe, stopping for a complimentary breakfast, only to be served a Jaffa orange grown in Israel. Much of the fruit Israel produces is shipped all over the world. Israel's reputation as a fruit producer is second to none, especially considering its minia-ture size and its great output of fruit, vegetables, and other foods. Once again, we have seen that the Bible is exactly true.

Looking at Israel's production record over the past 20 years, we begin to understand how much food has been grown in this area that once was desert. We can truly say the Bible's prediction of the deserts turning into the Garden of Eden have literally been fulfilled! However, the incredible story goes even further. Amos 9:13-14 says: *"Behold, the days come, saith the Lord, that the plowman shall overtake the reaper, and the treader of grapes him that soweth seed; and the mountains shall drop sweet wine, and all the hills shall melt. And I will bring again the captivity of my people of Israel, and they shall build the waste cities, and inhabit them; and they shall plant vineyards, and drink the wine thereof; they shall also make gardens, and eat the fruit of them."* Notice it makes a prediction there will be a day when the planter will overtake the reaper. Several years ago while visiting a farm in Israel, to my surprise I saw a man planting his seventh crop of the year while they were harvesting the sixth crop at the same time in the very same field! An exact fulfillment of what God predicted hundreds of years ago! We have watched God fulfill His promises as He said He would. The gardens, the farms, the fruit, and produce growing so lush in Israel, all point to the fact God makes promises and fulfills them exactly as He says.

Along with the increase of crops and farms in Israel, another very interesting development has been brought about. With the planting of trees and the increase of crops, has come a change in the climate of Israel. In the last 30 years, more than a 20 percent increase of rainfall has been recorded. As you might suspect, with an increase of rainfall and crops, there is also an increase in bugs. Along with the increase of bugs, there is also an increase of birds. The Bible also indicates the birds would be a sign for the last days. Revelation 19:17-18 says: *"And I saw an angel standing in the* sun; and he cried with a loud voice, saying to all the fowls that fly in the midst of heaven, Come and gather yourselves together unto the supper of the great God; That ye may eat the flesh of kings, and the flesh of captains, and the flesh of mighty men, and the flesh of horses, and of them that sit on them, and the flesh of all men, both free and bond, both small and great."

It is clear from the Bible that in a coming day at the Battle of Armageddon, the time period right between the Tribulation and the Kingdom of God, there will be a time when many birds will be present in Israel. These birds, such as buzzards, will come down to feed upon the bodies of kings and soldiers who will fight and be destroyed in the Battle of Armageddon. The Bible says there will be a great collection of these birds coming to feed on the bodies of men. Again, this prediction and sign from the Bible for the end days is substantiated by several interesting articles. For example, from the *Chicago Tribune* on April 6, 1986, there is an article entitled, "Israeli Pilots Battle Birds for Air Space." Here is what is says:

> "It happened during a routine training flight, the young Israeli pilot recalled. 'I was flying at about 3,000 feet when I suddenly heard a loud explosion and felt a strong blow on my neck. I completely blacked out.' The pilot regained consciousness a few seconds later to find his A-4 Skyhawk fighter hurling out of control, the wind roaring through his shattered canopy, and his neck covered with blood. 'I didn't know whether it was mine,' he said. 'I looked down. The floor was littered with feathers and torn flesh. I realized that I had collided with a bird.' It was a 20-pound pelican, and when it struck the jet, which was moving at 600 miles an hour, it hit the windshield with the force of 100 tons, tests later proved. The pilot managed to land his plane safely, but others

in the Israel Air Force have not been so lucky. There have been hundreds of collisions between birds and Israeli warplanes, killing some pilots and seriously injuring others and causing millions of dollars of damage in crashes, cracked wings, punctured fuselages, shattered canopies and destroyed engines, military officials say. The air force keeps detailed figures secret, but flight officers admit that since the 1973 Mideast War, pelicans, storks, and raptors (bird of prey) have downed and damaged more Israeli warplanes than all of the Arab air forces combined. Aircraft accidents caused by birds are a worldwide problem, but nowhere are they as frequent as in Israel. The distinction is created by the country's unique political and geographical situation. A tiny country whose relations with its neighbors are tense at best. Israel has one of the world's biggest air forces and littlest airspaces in which to train. That space happens to be along the main route for millions of birds seeking the shortest route around the Meditterranean Sea as they migrate between Europe, Western Asia, and Africa every spring and fall."

The article even goes on to say that in the month of May, over 620,000 honey buzzards flew right down the valley. As well, there were other kinds of birds of prey flying in the same valley at the same time. What a fulfillment of God's prophecy! The Bible predicted in the last days Israel would be regathered in the land, the deserts would bloom; and now we have seen that even the birds are coming back to the very place where the Bible predicts they will be. How exciting to see God fulfilling end-time prophecies in our own lifetime!

The stories of birds flying in Megiddo Valley, the very place where the Bible predicts the Battle of Armageddon will occur, is also documented in Israel's newspaper. In *The Jerusalem Post International Edition*, October 1, 1988, on page 9, is an article entitled, "Flying with the Birds." It says the birds are a menace to the air force and a mystery to bird watchers. As well, the *Jerusalem Post International Edition*, May 26, 1990, page 6, has an article entitled "Air Force Bows to Vultures Needs". It indicates the Israeli Air Force even had to quit flying during certain times of the year because the vultures were so thick. It is interesting where the the strategic air base in Israel is located--right in Megiddo Valley! How exciting to see every detail lined up exactly as the Bible predicted hundreds of years before.

All of this only reminds us of how we need to line up our lives with what the Bible has to say. How important it is for each of us to come to Christ and acknowledge that He alone is able to save us from our sin and qualify us for heaven by His shed blood and finished work on the cross. If you have not done so, why not at this very moment accept Him as your personal Savior? For those of you who do know Him, this is a time for us to begin living for Him. How thrilling to know Christ could come back for believers at any time. The question remains, **are you ready??**

Rebuilt Cities

As we consider our passage in Ezekiel 36:35 again, notice that the prediction of the end-time events concerning Israel does not end with just the blooming of the deserts. It also mentions there would be cities that had become wasted, desolate, ruined, but in the last days, they would become revitalized, fortified and lived in. Can we document this as well? I believe so! The fulfillment of Israel's rebuilt cities is not only interesting, but it is graphic as to how God is capable of fulfilling His Word even to the slightest detail. For example,

Amos 9:14 says: *"And I will bring again the captivity of my people of Israel, and they shall build the waste cities, and inhabit them; and they shall plant vineyards, and drink the wine thereof; they shall also make gardens, and eat the fruit of them."* This is a clear statement that wasted cities would be re-inhabited.

Zephaniah 2:4-7 not only mentions cities would become desolate, but it even mentions by name Ashdod, for destruction and rebuilding. Today Ashdod has been rebuilt and is Israel's largest deep-sea port! How amazing to see this being fulfilled. Ashkelon is another city the Bible said would be destroyed and rebuilt. Just as prophesied, Ashkelon today is a modern sea port with a population of more than 30,000 people. Are these and other cities which have been destroyed and rebuilt just an accident or did God really plan these to be a great sign? I believe they are a great fulfillment of exactly what God predicted through the prophets, Isaiah, Zephaniah, Jeremiah and Amos. We are certainly seeing God fulfill His Word in a great and marvelous way today.

Finally, listen to what Ezekiel is told in chapter 36:38: *"As the holy flock, as the flock of Jerusalem in her solemn feasts; so shall the waste cities be filled with flocks of men: and they shall know that I am the Lord."* Surely we have witnessed the ancient cities of Israel being destroyed and now rebuilt. For example, as we see Beer-Sheba's population exceed 100,000, we can't help but say what a thrill it is to see God's Word fulfilled. A number of people who frequently travel to Israel, also include in their list of the rebuilt and restored cities   Bethany, Bethel, Bethlehem, Cana, En-Gedi, Hebron, Jericho and Nazareth. What a testimony to the fulfillment of God's Word!

A Valley of Bones

God continues to describe Israel, in the latter days, to the prophet Ezekiel. In chapter 37, He does so by instructing the ancient prophet to walk through a valley filled with bones as stated in verses 1-4.

What a story this is. Many of us are familiar with the song entitled "Dry Bones". The setting for this old southern spiritual is quite significant. Can you imagine God asking Ezekiel to go to a valley of bones where He will communicate with him? I wonder how we would react? As Ezekiel walked through this graveyard, he noticed there were many bones and evidently life had departed from these bones long ago, for they were bleached by the weather and were dry. As a matter of fact, "very dry"! Then, God asked Ezekiel the question, "Can these bones live?" I know how I would have answered Him. I would have said, "There is no way! There is no way these bones will respond to anything I'm saying." But the prophet Ezekiel answers in a way showing he recognized the power of God, *"O Lord God, thou knowest."*

God then instructs Ezekiel to preach unto these bones. As Ezekiel begins to preach to the bones, they begin to wiggle in the dust. The toe bones joined to the foot bones, and the foot bones to the ankle bones, and the ankle bones to leg bones, and the leg bones to the back bones, and back bones to the neck and head bones. Finally, standing before him is a whole army of skeletons coming alive! Then, according to verses 6-7 of chapter 37, God puts flesh on the bones and breathes life into them. Standing before him, Ezekiel beholds quite a sight! Not only have the bones been resurrected, but they are becoming living people. Then verse 10 describes a great prophetic sign for the end days: *"So I prophesied as he commanded me, and the breath came into them, and they lived, and stood up upon their feet, an exceeding great army."*

Notice this verse says these bones which were at one time dead, are now resurrected, representing an exceeding great army. Can you name a time when Israel has ever been a great army? All throughout Israel's history, Israel has been picked on by its neighbors. It has only been in these last days that Israel's military has become a legend. Not too many years ago, the *Los Angeles Times* quoted Israel as being the fourth ranking major power in the world. When I drew this to the attention of an Israeli military man, he smiled and said, "We should be flattered to be numbered among powerful armies where the nations are so big." However, before he was done talking, I realized he had said this tongue in cheek, for he knew Israel's reputation and power as an army is really second to none throughout the world. This can be proven by the fact that since they became a nation in 1948, they have fought and won five wars, each time against insurmountable odds. There is no doubt in my mind that those of us alive today have seen God fulfill, in a literal way, this great sign. It has only been since Israel became a nation in 1948 that they have become a great, mighty, and powerful army! This is exactly the sign predicted by the Bible and told by God to the prophet Ezekiel.

Can you believe we are able to see such an incredible fulfillment of God's Word concerning Israel? Isn't the barren fig tree coming to life? Israel is back in the land, crops are growing in the desert, birds are flying in the valley prepared for battle. Destroyed cities have been rebuilt and Israel has become a great army. It certainly makes one stop and think that all of these events could not have happened by accident, but rather they are fulfillments by God, who is in control and knows all that is happening.

I have an entire collection of articles stating incredible facts concerning Israel's army and military power. One article indicates how modifications are made to various airplanes including the USAF "Wild Weasel" F-4G as well as the Skyhawk A-4. Israel has taken these planes from the United States and upgraded them! Upgraded planes have improved avionics and the capability which supports various new weapons systems for Israel. As well, I have documentation of how they have captured T-55, T-62, T-72 tanks and have installed updated weapons in them to make them fierce fighting components. These Soviet tanks were captured as Israeli armies defeated Arab forces coming against them. There are numerous articles with pictures showing a parade of SAM-5 missiles in Syria.

One article which I really enjoyed described a small artillery computer called DAVID. It is used to keep track of up to 28 enemy targets simultaneously. No wonder Israel has been so successful in five wars since they became a nation. Haven't we seen God provide a direct fulfillment of what the Bible said would take place in the latter days?

Israel as a Nation, A United Stick

But the signs and predictions concerning Israel don't stop. Notice Ezekiel 37:11 which predicts Israel will not only become a great army and be restored to their land, but as well they would even become a great nation. It is a remarkable statement to say Israel is back in the same land where once they dwelt long ago. It is even more remarkable to say they exist as a nation today against insurmountable odds and death threats on many sides. Today Israel is back in their own land and recognized as a nation by the majority of the world.

Furthermore, God told Ezekiel that when Israel came back as a nation, there would be another great miracle and sign pointing to the last days. This sign is documented in verses 16-17 in Ezekiel 37: *"Moreover, thou son of man, take thee one stick, and write upon it, for Judah, and for the children of Israel, his companions: then take another stick, and write upon it, For Joseph, the stick of Ephraim, and for all the house of Israel his companions: And join them one to another into one stick; and they shall become one in thine hand."*

I remember several years ago visiting with a leading Israeli official. He indicated we were living in the last days. He felt it was proper to be looking for the Messiah to come. While I agreed that we are living in the last days, I was interested in why he was so sure. He pointed specifically to these verses, and mentioned the fact that Israel has indeed become "one stick". What does it mean to be one stick? From the Bible's account 2,700 years ago, we are told that after King Saul, King David, and King Solomon, the nation of Israel divided into two parts, Judah and Israel. All the way from the days of Solomon until Israel was destroyed in A.D. 70, they were two sticks. But the Bible indicates in the last days when God is fulfilling His Word concerning Israel, these two sticks would be joined together and they would become one. In other words, Israel would become one nation again. Haven't we seen this take place in a literal fashion? For when Israel was reborn as a nation in 1948, they came back not as two nations--a separate Judah and Israel--but as one united nation! Again we have seen God's Word fulfilled exactly as He had said.

End-Time Enemies of Israel

Ezekiel 38-39 goes on to talk about another great sign of the latter days. As a matter of fact, verse 8 would suggest that this would probably not be fulfilled in Ezekiel's lifetime, but after "many days" and in the "latter years". The prophecy of these two chapters remains one of the great signs of the end times. According to the Bible, Ezekiel 38:2, in the latter days, Israel will be invaded by a country called the "chief prince". The actual Hebrew word for "chief prince" is *Rosh*. It also indicates that the capital of the principal cities of Rosh would be Meshech and Tubal. The study of history is interesting, for really, the word "Rosh" is our modern day word "Russia". There are two principal cities of Russia. Meshech, our modern-day Moscow, and Tubal, our modern-day Tubolsk.

Not only is Moscow the political capital of Russia, but Tubolsk is the industrial capital of Russia. Remember several years ago when Gary Powers, a U.S. pilot, was shot down while spying in a U-2 plane? He was shot down over the city of Tubolsk. The Bible says this invading force in the latter days will come from out of the north (Ezek. 38:15-16; 39:2). Could it be possible that Russia will invade Israel in the last days? I believe so. Even though we have seen many changes in Russia militarily, socially, and economically, the Bible's description and prediction is still clear. As a matter of fact, the Bible indicates that this would take place in the days after Israel had signed a peace treaty and put aside her weapons. According to verse 11 of chapter 38, Israel will be at rest, thinking it can dwell safely. This certainly doesn't describe Israel at the present time. Today Israel is armed and on alert. Daniel 9:27 indicates that there will be a day when Israel will sign a peace treaty and set down her weapons. It will be at this time the Russian invasion is predicted to take place.

But notice this. It also indicates the primary reason for the invasion will be, according to verses 12-13, three items which are described in Ezekiel 38:12-13:

Item Number One: Food

The Bible predicts Russia will be desperate for food. As we look at Russia today, we see how true this is. The people of Russia need physical food. Yet, there is an abundance of food in Israel. Crops are growing with record yields. Isn't it amazing that only recently Russia has found itself in a position of being desperate for food. And again, only recently, we have seen Israel's crops yielding in such a magnificent way.

Item Number Two: Money

The Bible also indicates it will be at a time when Russia needs money, as they will come to carry away "silver and gold". Again, we have witnessed the once powerful Russian nation come to a time when they are economically strapped. They have even come to the United States asking for a loan! They are beseeching the EEC for loans! At one time, a request was made for $250 billion from America. This in itself is amazing, considering that America is also in such poor financial shape. But the Bible indicates in a coming day they will see wealth in Israel, and Russia will invade to take advantage of both food and wealth.

Many have guessed this wealth might be the wealth of the Dead Sea. Others have thought it was due to commerce and trading. Some have thought it was due to the food products from Israel. Wherever the wealth comes from, we know this, there will be a day when Russia becomes desperate for money and Israel will appear to be rich with no military protection.

Item Number Three: People

It also implies that when Russia comes down, they will come to the desolate places--perhaps even the West Bank. There, they will seek to lay claim to some of the wealth and food because these are people who at one time inhabited the land of Russia. Isn't it interesting that the Russian Jews have settled on the West Bank! Could this be one of the reasons Russia will lay claim to going down against Israel in a coming day?

In addition, the Bible predicts that Russia will not come alone. According to Ezekiel 38:5-6, Iran (Persia), Ethiopia (Cush) and Libya (Put) will also come, all of them with their armies. The Bible also mentions in verse 6 that Germany

(Gomer) will come, having a united army! The whole world watched in amazement recently as the great Berlin Wall, dividing Germany, came tumbling down. In the 1970s and 1980s, if one approached the wall in Germany they would have been shot. Now, we have seen the wall destroyed and Germany is once again united. This is exactly the condition the Bible said would exist in the latter days, when Israel would be invaded by these armies.

The outcome of this invasion, however, is a disastrous one. The Bible mentions in chapter 39 that only one-sixth of the soldiers coming down against Israel will survive. Five-sixths will be destroyed by a series of events, including a great earthquake (Ezek. 38:19), mutiny, fighting among the invading armies themselves (38:21), pestilence and disease having to do with the blood (38:22), a flood (38:22), great hailstones, fire, and brimstones (38:22). When it is done, the entire world will recognize that Israel has been delivered from these great armies, even though they had set down all of their means of defense.

The warning should be given to the people of these countries to trust Christ now, for if they do, they will be part of the Rapture and they will not have to be a part of the devastation which will take place when God judges these armies. Surely it is a severe warning, but how much better to be warned than to walk into such calamity as described in God's Holy Word. This victory will remind Israel of their great deliverance out of Egypt. Remember, they escaped out of Egypt after being slaves for 400 years. After 400 years in slavery they had no army and they had no weapons, but God delivered them. So it will be when Russia and other armies of the world invade Israel. God will be their protection. Perhaps this will be the reason Israel begins to worship and sacrifice to God again. The nations described in Ezekiel 38 are existing today in exactly the way the Bible said they would. Again, we see another amazing fulfillment in Israel as a sign for the last days. We are reminded that each of us must be ready if Christ were to come today. These predictions by God made in the Bible hundreds of years ago, are not being fulfilled by accident. They are being fulfilled so you and I will know we are living in the last days.

Israel's Desire to Return to Sacrifice

No sign could be clearer concerning the last days than the sign of Israel returning to sacrifices. Look what the prophet Hosea records in chapter 3:4-5: *"For the children of Israel shall abide many days without a king, and without a prince, and without a sacrifice, and without an image, and without an ephod, and without teraphim: Afterward shall the children of Israel return, and seek the the Lord their God, and David their king; and shall fear the Lord and his goodness in the latter days."*

Notice the condition described in these verses is for "the latter days". Today we can say Israel has been without a king and without a sacrifice for many years. We have also seen them return to the land. Therefore, we know we must be living in the latter days. These verses also show Israel will be without a sacrifice for many years, but in the last days, things will change. Do you realize that in A.D. 70 when the Temple was destroyed in Israel, the sacrifices stopped? The Jews recognized the Romans were going to destroy the Temple. They took the artifacts out of the Temple and escaped down the Kidron Valley on the way to Masada. At Masada, they would make that gallant stand. After several years, the Romans would break through the fortress on top of Masada only to find the Jews had taken their own lives.

However, as the Jews went to Masada they thought that after a period of time the Romans would give up pursuing them. They thought once the Romans left they would be able to go back and retrace their steps to Jerusalem. They would then return to the caves where they had hidden artifacts from the Temple so they could begin their worship again. But since all the people but three were all killed on Masada, no one was left to retrieve the hidden artifacts. Now, many centuries later and particularly since Israel has become a nation, we have witnessed a number of caves in the Judean mountains yield incredible artifacts. Some of these artifacts date to the time of Herod's Temple and can be described as temple items.

It is also interesting that the prophet Daniel in Daniel 9:27 says: *"And he shall confirm the covenant with many for one week: and in the midst of the week he shall cause the sacrifice and oblation to cease, and for the overspreading of abominations he shall make it desolate, even until the consummation, and that determined shall be poured upon the desolate."*

This verse teaches that the Tribulation will begin when Israel signs a treaty confirming peace with an Antichrist. In other words, it is not the Rapture of the church that begins the Tribulation, but it is the signing of the treaty. I believe before the treaty is ever signed and the Antichrist is revealed, the church will be called home to heaven by Christ's coming in the clouds, giving a shout and the sounding of the trumpet. All true believers will then be caught up to be with Christ. This is described in 1 Thessalonians 4:16-18. It is a glorious event for those who are believers in Jesus Christ.

Notice also the Bible teaches that in the middle of this seven-year period, introduced by the signing of a treaty, the Antichrist will break the treaty and demand the sacrifices cease. If the Antichrist is going to stop the sacrifices in the middle of the seven-year period, then sometime between now and the middle of the seven-year period, sacrifices must *begin!* We have already seen that since A.D. 70 no animal sacrifices have taken place. However, there is no item of greater interest to Israel than the re-institution of animal sacrifices. As Israel plans these animal sacrifices (and today they are), isn't it amazing we are seeing one more great sign that we must be living in the latter days.

Amos 9:11 says the Tabernacle of David will be raised up in the latter years. Acts 15:16 says the Lord will build "again the Tabernacle of David". It is exciting that both references mention the Tabernacle and not the Temple. Remember, the Tabernacle where David worshipped was not a stone building. As well, remember the Tabernacle was composed of sheets of materials and skins of animals. It would be possible to erect such a Tabernacle within hours. In other words, once Israel decides they want to sacrifice and worship Jehovah, within hours they could do so in this very manner! The Bible says this will take place in the latter days. Even though sacrifices have not taken place for almost 1,900 years, there is an interest in resuming these sacrifices again! As such, it is a direct fulfillment of end-time Bible prophecy.

The Jerusalem Post International Edition, December 30, 1989, pages 9-11, provides an article entitled, "Speedily, In Our Time?". It is an article describing the desire and intent of the Jewish people to rebuild a house to worship the Lord. It is interesting, because along with the rebuilding of the Tabernacle, they mention resuming animal sacrifices. One of the sub-sections of this article is entitled, "In Search of the Red Heifer." What a story the ashes of the red heifer is!

It begins in Numbers 19 with the instructions to Moses about taking an animal, a heifer, that is pure red and has no blemish. It is one of the few sacrifices where the sex of the animal is stated as a heifer, or a female. It is one of the few sacrifices where the color of the animal is also specified--red.

This was to be a unique and rare sacrifice. It is a great picture of Christ, since He also was a unique and special sacrifice. But even more important in Numbers 19:21, it records it was to be a perpetual sacrifice. Ideally, this sacrifice was to be done only one time. We read in Hebrews 9-10 that Christ also was offered up only one time. In other words, only *one time* Christ died for the sin of the whole world. How wonderful to know His death and resurrection are still payment for anyone who will turn to Christ and accept Him as their personal Savior by putting their faith in Him.

The story of the ashes of the red heifer is a very interesting one. In this ancient sacrifice they would take the animal outside the city. First, they would make a pot using the manure from the animal mixed with clay. This pot was called a *kalal*, and when the animal was entirely burned, the ashes were put into the pot. Using a long reed, they would dip the end of the reed into the pot of ash, and then dip the reed into a basin of water. If there was a house where a death occurred, or contagious diseases were present, the inhabitants were pronounced unclean and had to leave the city. Once outside the city, they would be inspected by the priest. If they were cleared to go back into the city, the priest would sprinkle them with the mixture of water and ash from the basin. Now the priest would be unclean until evening, according to Numbers 19, but the people could go back into the city. We can see how this is a marvelous picture of Christ, for Hebrews 13:11 says He would suffer outside the camp. 2 Corinthians 5:21 also indicates: *"For he hath made him to be sin for us, who knew no sin; that we might be made the righteousness of God in him."*

What a transaction was made on Calvary. I was a sinner and He took my sin. He was righteous and He gave me His righteousness. This is why God can accept a sinner who comes to Christ for forgiveness and salvation. I believe the sacrifice of the ashes of the red heifer is one of the most picturesque examples of what actually took place on Calvary.

But to complete our story concerning current events, it is interesting to note a number of people feel that presently the Jews are on the verge of discovering these ashes. The search is being carried on by several groups. The most promising appears to be the group digging right in the Qumran area of Israel. This is also in the exact area where other great discoveries of artifacts dating from the Temple days have been found. Though they have not found the ashes, they have discovered many clues indicating they may be digging in the right spot! How exciting to see in Israel's own newspaper, they are talking of beginning the sacrifices once again. How interesting to see that the headlines actually talk about the breeding of the red heifer.

Time magazine, October 16, 1989, pages 64-66, has an grand article entitled, "Time for a New Temple". It mentions that many of the Jews believe it may be time to rebuild the Temple. They also believe that it may be time to restore sacrifices. The *Time* article lists three problems. One problem is knowing who the priest might be. However, they now know of schools that are training students on the elaborate details of Temple service. Other questions raised include where these sacrifices will take place and the location of the original site of the Temple. Recently, however, more and more people, Jews and Gentiles alike, are convinced that the exact location of the ancient Temple was to the north of the Dome of the Rock. Therefore, the Dome of the Rock might not have to be moved at all for sacrifices to begin! Instead, if you line up the East Gate (actually, the East Gate of Jesus' day would be beneath the present ground level and slightly to the south) and a recently discovered Herodian Gate, it is easy to fix the location of the Temple just north of the Dome of the Rock.

Now *Time* magazine indicates that only one difficulty remains: *"One difficulty is the requirement (as in Num. 19:1-10) that priests purify their bodies with the cremated ashes of an unblemished red heifer before they enter the Temple. Following a go-ahead from the Chief Rabbinate, institute operatives spent two weeks in August scouting Europe for heifer embryos which will shortly be implanted into cows at an Israeli cattle ranch."* This is truly amazing. Even *Time* magazine indicates that the Jews are excited about restoring sacrifices. But isn't this what the Bible predicted? Wasn't this a sign for the latter days? Didn't Hosea 3:4-5 indicate that in the latter days when Israel would return to the land, sacrifices which had been stopped would be restored?

On one of my recent visits to Israel, I had the pleasure of visiting the Temple Institute. It is located in the Jewish Quarter of the Old City of Jerusalem. What a fascinating time to meet dedicated Jews who are seeking to rebuild items identical to the ones which were used in ancient Temple rituals. Altogether, over 93 sacred Temple items have been constructed from gold, silver and copper. These people are excited about seeing Temple worship restored because they recognize approximately one-third of the 613 biblical laws they feel committed to obey are dependent on the presence of a Temple in Jerusalem! As a result, the Temple Institute has set itself to the task of laying the educational foundation for the observance of these laws. For years the Temple Institute has researched the materials, the measurements, the forms of these sacred vessels. Now construction is under way!

Actually, this is an ancient dream. The Temple Institute's magazine entitled, *The Treasure of the Temple*, pages 2-3, says:
"News, at once began rebuilding it. King Herod glorified it. For

almost 1,000 years the Temple was the religious, historical, political, legal, and cultural center of the Jewish nation. People came from all over the world to see the service of the white-robed priests of Israel in the House of the God of Jacob. The dream of rebuilding the Temple spans 50 generations of Jews, five continents and innumerable seas and oceans. The prayer for rebuilding is recited in as many languages as are known to humanity. These prayers recited in prisons and ghettos, studying halls and synagogues, homes and fields everyday for 2,000 years of exile, in the face of poverty and persecution and seemingly hopeless peril, now gain a new dimension with the return of the people of Israel to the Land of Israel, with the rebirth of a Jewish state and the creation of a Jewish army and the flowering of the desert and the scientific and social strides made by the nation of Israel. This new dimension is: a Possibility."

How interesting to see the Jews feel that the time during which those sacrifices were made is nothing more than a parenthesis in history! How exciting to see they feel it is now time to restore not only the Temple, but also the sacrifices.

The Temple Institute has even produced postcards showing a red heifer, and on the back, quoting Numbers 19! In their shop they also have postcards of a number of other items including harps, the silver trumpets, the silver decanter, the lyre, the golden *mezerak* used for carrying blood to the altar, and the silver *makheth* used for removing ashes from the altar in the morning. At the present time, work is going on to construct a golden *menorah*. Do you see how serious these Jews are with regard to returning to sacrifices again? After all, how can they obey God and please a coming Messiah if approximately one-third of their 613 laws are dependent upon the presence of a Temple in Jerusalem? If they do not begin sacrificing again in the Temple, they would disobey the commandments of God in over 200 of these laws.

Other articles in the Jewish paper include headlines such as, "On the Trail of a Holy Cow", which reports a man seeking to use genetic engineering to produce kosher red heifers required for Temple sacrifices. This article appeared in *The Jerusalem Post International Edition* on August 19, 1989. While some believe they must find the original ashes of the red heifer, as hidden in the hillside from the destruction of the Temple in A.D. 70, others claim the process could be started again with a new red heifer! Only time will tell which faction is right. In the meantime, all of us can say we are seeing the Bible fulfilled with amazing accuracy.

Recently on one of my trips to Israel, I was amazed when my Israeli guide, who has become a good personal friend, pointed out a sign to me. On the pathway leading from the Wailing Wall (Western Wall) to the Temple Mount is a sign written in three languages. The message is from the Chief Rabbi of Israel. It states, *"According to Jewish law, it is strictly forbidden for anyone to enter the Temple Mount owing to its sanctity."* After a discussion and a visit to one of the caves where they are actually digging for the ashes of the red heifer, my Israeli guide pointed to this sign and said, "When they find the ashes, they will be able to remove this sign." In other words, they will be able to restore the priesthood and begin animal sacrifices again. Once this has been done, Jews can be purified and can go on the Temple Mount again. Just a few years ago, these things were unheard of in Israel. Now this news makes the headlines in their papers. Surely we are watching God fulfill His Word in an amazing way.

The Barren Fig Tree Coming to Life

Remember we said Israel was portrayed as a fig tree? I believe that fig tree was withered up because it bore no spiritual fruit in the days of Christ. When the disciples asked

Christ what would be a sign of the end of the age, and when would these things all be fulfilled, He indicated the sign would be when they saw the tree that was withered, restored to health again. Notice Christ didn't say the tree would be bearing fruit, but rather that its branches would be young and tender. Therefore, Israel would be a national and political reality, but not necessarily responding to Christ spiritually. Wouldn't you say the nation born in 1948 was a young and tender nation? Haven't we seen Israel, just like a withered and barren fig tree, come back to life in full bloom? This fig tree has been restored to the land. Crops are growing in the desert. Cities have been rebuilt. Israel has a great army. It has become a nation. It has become united as one nation. Its enemies are identified and poised, and now Israel even stands ready to sacrifice! All of these are direct fulfillments of what the Bible said would take place with Israel in the latter days. Surely the generation that sees Israel restored as a nation is the generation which Jesus spoke about.

But if this generation is the time frame that Christ spoke about, how long is the generation? This question has been asked by many for years. Some people claim that a generation is 40 years. While the Bible does mention the 40-year generation, the Bible also mentions a generation can be 33 years, or in one case, 70 years. As a matter of fact, in Genesis 15:13-16, we read of a generation that averages 100 years. A generation is not a specific amount of time. Rather, it is a variable time used by God for working with a nation, a family, or an individual. While we don't know how long a generation is, it does appear that the fulfillment of Christ's Words will take place during the lifetime of those who see all of these great signs take place.

You and I are among the people alive today who have seen the barren fig tree come to life. We have seen Israel replanted as a nation. We have seen the Bible's great prophecies fulfilled. If there is ever a people who should be aware that we are living in the last days, it should be us. What better time than now to confess our need of a Savior to God. To repent and turn from our sin and to receive Jesus Christ as our blessed Savior. His blood alone is sufficient to take away our sin. It is through no work which we can do; it isn't even enough to pray. The Bible simply says we should believe in Him. To those who believe in Him and take the death of Christ as a substitute payment for their sin, God has promised He would give them eternal life. John 3:36 says: *"He that believeth on the Son hath everlasting life: and he that believeth not the Son shall not see life; but the wrath of God abideth on him."*

Why remain in the second part of the verse and be eternally lost when, because of Christ's death and resurrection, you can be on your way to heaven? Place your trust in Christ right now.

The New World Order In Bible Prophecy

When President Bush made his first speech concerning the Gulf War at the National Religious Broadcasters Convention in Washington, D.C., to an audience of about 4,000, the president presented his stand on the war, and then went on to say, "You know what is going to solve all of our problems? There is something new called the New World Order. When this comes in, it's going to bring peace like we have never seen. We are going to be able to lay down all of our weapons. The New World Order is the solution to all of our problems."

Most of the several thousand religious broadcasters stood and applauded the president. Only a dozen or so people remained seated. Stunned, they wondered, as I did, "Can this really be happening?"

Many who heard that speech did not realize the significance of the president's words. But those of us who have studied biblical prophecy knew George Bush was articulating, for the first time in a public forum, what we knew would come to pass some day.

The New World Order will indeed bring the world together under one government, but it will create more problems than it will solve. In fact, in the end this New World Order will neatly give its power to the Antichrist exactly as the Bible predicted hundreds of years ago.

What is an antichrist? It is one who will pretend to be

everything for which Christ stands, but he will be the exact opposite. So, he is anti-christ because he is really opposed to Christ. He will pretend he is the Christ, hoping to win the affection of people.

The Bible says there will come a time when there will be one-world government with one economic system under the control of one man. Scripture says there will be a revived Roman Empire that will rule for a short time. Then, people will give their allegiance to this Antichrist for the rest of time.

These predictions were given to the prophet Daniel some 2,500 years ago; and to the Apostle John some 1,900 years ago. Bible prophecy is different from the predictions found at the grocery tabloid counter--those predictions were made last week with most of them never coming true. The Bible's predictions were made hundreds of years ago, and every one of them will come true; not some, but all of them!

The Royal Nightmare

One night, about 2,500 years ago, King Nebuchadnezzar had a nightmare. After tossing and turning, he sat up in bed and said, "I have just had this royal dream, and I know it is important because if *I* dreamed it, it *has* to be important. Nothing but important things go through my mind."

He called for the royal wise men and demanded they tell him the royal interpretation of his royal dream. "If you will tell us the royal dream, Your Highness, we will make up the royal lie; we mean the royal interpretation," they replied. The king interrupted them. "As a matter of fact, I've been meaning to talk to you about that. I tell you my dreams, and you guys make up these interpretations that never come true. If you are so smart, you figure out what I dreamed and then the meaning of it, too!" "Oh, no!" they quickly reminded him.

"That's not in our royal contract."

The king responded, "I tell you what. If you can't figure out the dream and give me its interpretation, I am going to cut off your heads." (This threat was extended to the prophet Daniel, too.) Now, Daniel was a Hebrew, who, as a teenager, had been taken from his home in Jerusalem and transported some 800 miles away to the conquering Babylonians. When he was brought to this foreign kingdom, they tried to change his name, his language, and his diet. He said, "Wait a minute! You will have to excuse me, but you see, I'm a Jewish boy. There are certain things a Jewish boy doesn't eat or drink. If you don't mind, I'll have my own food, and I will eat that instead." "Oh, Daniel," the king urged, "when in Babylon, do as the Babylonians do." But Daniel refused that generous invitation. Since Daniel was not afraid to take a stand, God blessed him. God is still looking for young people who will take a stand. If they do, He will bless them. God delights in blessing people.

When Daniel heard about the execution notice, he went to King Nebuchadnezzar and said, "Would it be okay, before you chop our heads off, if I pray to my God?" The king answered, "Sure, you can pray." Daniel had more freedom to pray in a foreign language than we do in our public schools today! Isn't that pathetic? But, it is true. I don't know if you believe in prayer or not, but I believe my God hears and answers prayer.

I remember a story about a young man who was going to study medicine. He went to a university where there was a noted chemistry teacher who hated Christians. Every year, the professor would ask if there were any Christians in the class. If someone was brave enough to admit to being a Christian, he would have them stand up. "You pray to your God that as I drop this beaker, it will not break when it hits the floor," he would say. Of course, everyone would laugh, and no one would stand up and pray. One semester, a young Christian man who was studying to be a doctor found himself in the atheist's chemistry class. A few days into the semester, the professor came in and asked, "Is there anyone here who is a Christian?" The young man raised his hand, and the professor told him to stand up. When asked if he believed in prayer, the student responded, "Yes, sir." The professor said, "Well then, I want you to pray to your God that when I drop this beaker, it won't break." As everyone else in class began to laugh and snicker, the young man bowed his head and prayed out loud. When he was through, the professor dropped the beaker. Because this atheist was so nervous about having had someone pray in his class, when he dropped the beaker, it fell, hit his toe, and then rolled onto the floor without breaking. The professor was laughed right out of his classroom. You see, I believe in a God to whom you can pray, and so did this young man.

The Head of Gold

Daniel prayed, and God told him the king's dream and its interpretation! The next day, Daniel went back into the king's presence and said, "Listen, king, I think I know what you saw in your vision. You saw a huge image with its top made of gold." Amazed, the king admitted that was his dream. "How did you know?" he asked. Daniel replied that his God had revealed the dream to him and went on to tell the king the rest of the dream.

"After the head of gold, there was a chest and arms of silver. The belly and thighs were of bronze with legs of iron. The feet were part iron and part clay. They were extensions of the legs, but clay had been mingled with the iron." The king was in astonishment, "That is exactly what I saw!"

Daniel continued with the dream. "You then saw a stone that looked as if it came out of the mountain, but it was not cut with hands. As it came, it rolled toward the image and crushed it. In fact, it ground the image into powder. The stone then began to grow until it filled the entire earth." The bewildered king then said, "That's exactly what I saw! But, what does it mean?"

Daniel said, "All right, here is the interpretation, and it is a sure one. If my God could show me the dream, then His interpretation of it is sure." He then said, *"Thou, O King, art the head of gold."* Nebuchadnezzar liked this interpretation. Frankly, I don't think he heard another word Daniel said. I believe he thought, *Wow! I am the head of gold...that's me. That's me, all right, way up there on the top!*

What did he do? He built a golden image to himself and placed it in the plain of Shinar. As everyone came from all over the world, they would bow down to the golden image of him. Yes, he liked that interpretation.

Daniel, however, told him, "God said you are not going to be the king forever. You are going to be replaced by another country that is inferior to you. It will be the silver. After it will come another, even more inferior nation, and it will take over the world. It will be the bronze. Then, there will be another part with two legs of iron that will be yet another kingdom. Finally, at the end of time, there will be ten toes. They are part iron and part clay; and they are going to be an extension of those iron legs, even though they will be another kingdom. However, this kingdom will rule only a little while. A stone will come and crush all of it. This stone will begin a kingdom of which there will be no end."

This stone is none other than the Kingdom of God. Remember, when Christ begins to rule and reign, He will rule forever.

The Ram and the Goat

Let's look at Daniel's prophecies concerning the two world empires that were to follow King Nebuchadnezzar's Babylonian Empire: "*And after thee shall arise another kingdom inferior to thee, and another third kingdom of brass, which shall bear rule over all the earth*" (Dan. 2:39).

These kingdoms have come into reality, exactly as the Bible said. In the book of Daniel, not one time, but four times, God described every world power, in order, and called them by name. In order to understand their significance, look at what Daniel 8:3-8 says: "*Then I lifted up mine eyes, and saw, and, behold, there stood before the river a ram which had two horns: and the two horns were high; but one was higher than the other, and the higher came up last. I saw the ram pushing westward, and northward, and southward; so that no beasts might stand before him, neither was there any that could deliver out of his hand; but he did according to his will, and became great. And as I was considering, behold, an he goat came from the west on the face of the whole earth, and touched not the ground: and the goat had a notable horn between his eyes. And he came to the ram that had two horns, which I had seen standing before the river, and ran unto him in the fury of his power. And I saw him come close unto the ram, and he was moved with choler against him, and smote the ram, and brake his two horns: and there was no power in the ram to stand before him, but he cast him down to the ground, and stamped upon him: and there was none that could deliver the ram out of his hand. Therefore the he goat waxed very great: and when he was strong, the great horn was broken; and for it came up four notable ones toward the four winds of heaven.'*

After the head of gold, which was Nebuchadnezzar's Babylon, the kingdom of the Medes and the Persians became the next world power. The two arms represent the two parts of their kingdom. In verse 20 Daniel writes, "*The ram which*

thou sawest having two horns are the kings of Media and Persia."
Like a lopsided ram with one horn bigger than the other, the
Persian Empire would come up last and be the dominant
power. Just as Daniel predicted, that is exactly what happened.

The third kingdom, represented in this vision as the
mean he-goat with one horn, beat up the ram with two horns,
and the he-goat began to rule the world. This is the Grecian
Empire seen as the belly and thighs of bronze in the king's
dream. Then, when the he-goat was in his prime--in his great
fury--the big horn broke, and four horns popped out of his
head. The kingdom represented by the he-goat was that of
Alexander the Great, the dominant king of Greece who died
in his prime. His four generals took power after him. Look at
verse 21: *"And the rough goat is the king of Grecia: and the great
horn that is between his eyes is the first king."* Isn't that pretty
simple? That is Alexander the Great.

Alexander the Great conquered the world when he was
barely 30 years old, and then became frustrated because
there was nothing else to conquer. Instead, he went around
the world putting on marching exhibitions. He caught a marsh
fever and died a fool's death while putting on a parade. His
generals came home to his infant son to say, "Your daddy's
dead, now you rule the world." The son asked, "What do I
do with the world?" It is recorded that the four generals of
Alexander the Great killed his son and divided the kingdom
among themselves.

Consider what the Bible said 175 years before Alexander
the Great was ever born! Verses 21 and 22 state: "...*and the
great horn that is between his eyes is the first king. Now that being
broken, whereas four stood up for it, four kingdoms shall stand up
out of the nation, but not in his power."* These verses refer to
Alexander the Great, and the last verse tells us that his son

would not rule after him. Isn't the Bible clear? The head of gold is Babylon; the arms and chest of silver are the Medes and the Persians; and the belly and thighs of bronze are none other than Alexander the Great.

These empires are recorded in yet another manner. Daniel described them as three animals: the first one, like a lion with eagle's wings (Babylon); next, a bear with three ribs in his mouth (the Medo-Persians--this is a matter of recorded history); and third, a leopard with four wings that depict the swiftness of Alexander the Great's world conquest.

The Fourth Kingdom

What about the fourth kingdom? In the interpretation of the king's dream, Daniel wrote: "*And the fourth kingdom shall be strong as iron: forasmuch as iron breaketh in pieces and subdueth all things: and as iron that breaketh all these, shall it break in pieces and bruise. And whereas thou sawest the feet and toes, part of potters' clay, and part of iron, the kingdom shall be divided; but there shall be in it of the strength of the iron, forasmuch as thou sawest the iron mixed with miry clay. And as the toes of the feet were part of iron, and part of clay, so the kingdom shall be partly strong, and partly broken. And whereas thou sawest iron mixed with miry clay, they shall mingle themselves with the seed of men: but they shall not cleave one to another, even as iron is not mixed with clay. And in the days of these kings shall the God of heaven set up a kingdom, which shall never be destroyed: and the kingdom shall not be left to other people, but it shall break in pieces and consume all these kingdoms, and it shall stand for ever. Forasmuch as thou sawest that the stone was cut out of the mountain without hands, and that it brake in pieces the iron, the brass, the clay, the silver, and the gold; the great God hath made known to the king what shall come to pass hereafter: and the dream is certain, and the interpretation thereof sure* "(Dan. 2:40-45).

What kingdom do the legs of iron represent? The Roman Empire with its two capitals: Rome and Constantinople. How do we know? Revelation 17:10 tells us that seven kings will rule the world. The first two were Assyria and Egypt. Then Daniel comes in chronologically with Babylon as number three. The fourth and fifth kingdoms were the Medes and the Persians, followed by Alexander the Great. In verses 10-13 we find: "*And there are seven kings: five are fallen, and one is, and the other is not yet come; and when he cometh, he must continue a short space. And the beast that was, and is not, even he is the eighth, and is of the seven, and goeth into perdition. And the ten horns which thou sawest are ten kings, which have received no kingdom as yet; but receive power as kings one hour with the beast. These have one mind, and shall give their power and strength unto the beast.*"

The Bible says, "*...five are fallen, one is....*" Who would be in power when Revelation was written at about A.D. 95 or A.D. 96?--Rome. This passage states there are seven kings; five are fallen, one is right now, and the other will come later. The last kingdom will be an extension of the iron legs that Daniel wrote about. It will be a revived Roman Empire. It will be part iron and part clay, a mixture of religion and politics. In Daniel 7:7-8 we read: "*After this I saw in the night visions, and behold a fourth beast, dreadful and terrible, and strong exceedingly; and it had great iron teeth: it devoured and brake in pieces, and stamped the residue with the feet of it: and it was diverse from all the beasts that were before it; and it had ten horns. I considered the horns, and, behold, there came up among them another little horn, before whom there were three of the first horns plucked up by the roots: and, behold, in this horn were eyes like the eyes of man, and a mouth speaking great things.*"

In verse 7, Daniel said he saw a beast so terrible, it was like nothing he had ever seen before. This dreadful, ugly beast was so strong that it had great iron teeth (like the iron legs). It broke all the other kingdoms. Ten horns then came up representing ten kings--in other words, an extension of those legs would be the feet, part of iron and part of clay.

The Revived Roman Empire

The Bible states what has and is going to happen. There will be Babylon; the Medes and the Persians; Greece and Alexander the Great; the Roman Empire; and then an extension of one--a revived Roman Empire with ten horns or ten kings. Once this last kingdom comes to power, it will rule for one hour, and then will give its power to the beast. He will rule and make war against the Lamb.

An article in the *Wichita Eagle* stated, *"...Since the fall of the Roman Empire, there has been the dream of a unified Europe. We are...seeing a brand new Roman Empire reconstructed."* Even news reporters call the unified Europe the new Roman Empire.

On December 31, 1992, the European Economic Community took power, and on January 1, 1993, its policies went into effect. Until recently, the European Community was considered to be only a political coalition. Now, it has gone from an economic dream to a political reality.

The *Kansas City Star* recently ran an article, "Is Euro-man Kinda' Like Superman?" It goes on to state that most of western Europe will be combined into one big, powerful, economic unit that will be the envy of the world.

Will it work? Will it dominate America? Will America be second class? The answer is yes. The European Community is on the verge of becoming the dominant power of the world. It is a revived Roman Empire. *Northwest Magazine*, sponsored by an airline, carried an article declaring that America will take a back seat to the revived Roman Empire.

After the Persian Gulf Crisis, I flew back from Israel and landed in Greece. I was handed a card stating that any person who is a citizen of any one of the twelve Common Market nations would not have to fill out any legal papers when going from one country to another in Europe. However, any person who is not from one of the Common Market nations would have to fill out all of the papers.

Forbes Magazine wrote: *"There will only be one Europe. It will be a super power."*

Will there be one currency, or many? This magazine answers: *"Ultimately, the move to a single currency is about symbolism and power. There will be only one economy, and it will not only be a united Europe, but it will probably be a united world."*

In the business section of the previously quoted European newspaper, there is a very interesting second section depicting what Europeans describe as a historical moment-- "Making History, A Unique Moment As World Leaders Gather In London." Why? To launch the first test for the Euro-bank and the new Euro-dollar. It's already here; it's already been issued; and now, it's on its way.

The New World Order

How close are we to the New World Order? An article in the *Atlantic Journal* begins by announcing a New World Order--a world quite different from the one we have known--with a United Nations that performs as envisioned by its founders. It goes on to say that following the Persian Gulf Crisis, the New World Order is emerging as our only hope for peace around the world.

This is it. Utopia. It is finally here, bringing the nations of the world under one government. If we have one government, we will have no wars, they say. This deceptive promise of heaven on earth is winning great popularity. Howard

Wilkins, an ambassador to one of the Common Market nations said, *"We will not recognize the world because of the change militarily and politically in Europe. Once it is united, it will be as big or bigger than the United States in terms of its marketing power."*

He is right. Soon we may not recognize the world. The truthful observer must agree that America is in decay. A new superstar is on the scene--a united Europe--a revived Roman Empire exactly as the Bible said. The Common Market says to the industrialized nations, "Hey, the United States is in decline. If you want to look at the future, you'd better align with the Common Market--the seat of world power."

Presently, there are twelve countries in the Common Market with several others who want in. Do you know what is so interesting about that? The Bible states that when the Antichrist comes to power, he will pull three nations out. Then he will put himself in power, allowing only ten nations to remain. Now, if he is going to pull out three and leave ten, that means he will have begun with thirteen. In a special edition of the *Jerusalem Post*, which featured the twelve stars of the Common Market nations, guess which nation the *Post* was recommending for number thirteen? The Israeli Star of David! Entering Europe's charmed circle seems to be Israel's goal.

The Lady and the Tower of Babel

The cover of the book *Europe Is Rising* pictures the tower of Babel, a symbol commonly used by the Common Market, and includes these words, *"Europe, many tongues, one voice."* In the background, a modern crane leans against the ancient tower. In addition, the twelve stars of the Common Market are inverted, converting them into the sign of Satan. Just coincidence?

Canadian television aired a two-hour special called "Europe Unbounded," in which a United Europe was predicted to rule the world while the United States and Canada would be left powerless. During the program, some of the symbols of the United Europe were shown, including the tower of Babel and the image of a woman. Why are these symbols so important? According to the Bible, the last world political system will be composed part of iron and part of clay. What do these two parts represent?

Revelation 17 says that in the last days there will be a prostitute, a harlot, and she will commit fornication. She (religion) will sell herself to the kings of the world. In other words, religion and politics will join together. Why? To bring all men under one single government and one single religion.

What will be the foundation of this world religion? The New Age movement--the fastest growing religion in America today. In fact, it has already infiltrated churches, businesses, the media, sports, and even our schools. Children can learn how to visualize and have out-of-body experiences; they can be hypnotized; but they cannot pray to the God of all creation.

The present unity movement, under the guise of the New Age movement, is none other than the plan of the Antichrist and Satan. To understand how the world could be fooled into believing the lies of this satanic religion, we need to go back to the tower of Babel, where the New Age had its beginnings.

In Genesis 11 we read of an unnamed people building a great city on the plain of Shinar. To the narrator of this parable, peering across time and desert from his nomadic traditions, these folks were awesomely clever. Since they all spoke one common language, nothing was impossible for them. The plan of these ingenious people was to erect a huge tower whose top would reach to heaven. It would be an altar to their own intellect called Babel, or Gate of God. Their idea was to build a tower to God, to reach up and touch Him, so they, too, would become gods. The religion of Nimrod and Babel taught that we are all gods. An advertisement that appeared in the *Wall Street Journal* concerned the ancient tower of Babel and was presented as a parable. The ad stated: *"Babel or Gate of God, the God himself came down. Walked the streets of their cities, saw their project under construction. The arrogant race angered him. He passed his hand over the city, cursed it, now where there had been one language, suddenly there were hundreds. Confusion reigned. Nothing was possible."* The ad said the lesson taught by this ancient parable is uncannily applicable for us in the 20th century. They are saying, "Listen, people, we have got to get together." Get it? If we can come together--if we can have one common language, government, and religion--nothing will be impossible for us.

Revelation 17 said in the last days there will be a harlot, a prostitute, who will sit on a beast; and she will ride across all the world. She will represent a religion that will bring everyone together. The harlot (the end-time religious system) will sit on the beast (the Antichrist and his end-time dictatorship), and she will ride around the world collecting all peoples into one.

The Bible says that the harlot, the woman, will ride a beast. I used to think this parading harlot was just an accident until I ran across the front cover of the June 1975 edition of *European Official Magazine*. Even then, it showed a Roman goddess riding on a beast as one of the official symbols of the Common Market. Accident? Not at all. One of the first stamps put out by the Common Market--a collective stamp used for the entire Common Market--showed the god of Europe riding on the back of a bull, begging to be worshipped.

This is an exact picture of Revelation 17. The Bible says that when Europe finally gets to the position where it has all the power--economically, politically, and religiously--it will have but a short time to live. The New World Order will rule only one hour and will give its power, strength, and might to the beast.

The Antichrist

Telemarketing Magazine ran an article addressing the future of Europe. Is Europe actually going to unite and work together in a unified form? The article states, *"I think it remains to be seen, but if it is going to work, a united Europe will need a leader. Yes, only one overall leader to function effectively. If they are going to work, they will have to have one man who will head up the entire thing."*

George Will, of the *Shreveport Journal*, writes, "Europe Moving Toward a Bureaucratic State." You know what? He is right.

Mr. Will goes on to say, "When I was in Washington, D.C. in early 1991, I saw a long line of limousines snaking down the street in front of one of the city's plush hotels. I asked a chauffeur who the dignitary was. 'Ah,' he said, 'it is the president of Europe.' The president of Europe? I didn't know they had one. I discovered that he is not really as much of a potentate as his title implies or as he plans to be. But there is a president of Europe who is appointed, not elected, to bring about a political unity in Europe and around the world. He has 15,000 employees to help him."

In Europe last year, I picked up a copy of a European newspaper. The front page read, "The New Mr. Europe." It stated that he will take over the presidency in January 1993, at what (in theory) will be the dawn of a new Europe. It will be a time when Europe will dominate and control the world.

Before all these events fully take place, the trumpet is going to sound, and all true believers are going to be taken out of this world. How do I know? Because the Bible says that is exactly what is going to happen.

I really believe we are living near the end of time. If we are the people who are going to see the last political system, then the system cannot take over and rule until the church is gone. We may see this last empire beginning to form, but it will not fully be in place until after the Rapture of the church. That's why we as Christians must be different from any other people who have ever lived before. Jesus could come today to take every born-again person home to heaven.

When the Antichrist makes his appearance, he will speak great, swelling words of promise. I believe there will be people, maybe even someone reading this book, who will attend that first unholy Sunday. You and others may say after the great disappearing of the true church, "Something is going on, and I have to find out what it is." The great orator, the Antichrist, will have magnificent, thrilling explanations for the disappearance of the millions of true Christians.

This tremendous, worldwide religious movement will bring all people into a single religion, and some into one government with one economy exactly as prophesied in God's Word. The Apostle John saw two beasts. The first beast came out of the sea, that is, out of the Gentile world powers. *"I...saw a beast rise up out of the sea, having seven heads and ten horns, and upon his horns ten crowns, and upon his heads the name of blasphemy"* (Rev. 13:1). The one who appears is the Antichrist. He will come up out of the kingdoms of the Gentiles.

The False Prophet
Just as there is a true Trinity, there is a false trinity. There

is God, the Father; God, the Son; and God, the Holy Spirit. Satan's trinity puts him in the place of God; the Antichrist in the place of Jesus Christ; and an anti-prophet (or anti-spirit) in the place of the Holy Spirit.

In Revelation 13, we are introduced to this false prophet. It appears to me that he comes up out of the land of Israel because in verse 11 we find, *"And I beheld another beast coming up out of the earth; and he had two horns like a lamb, and he spake as a dragon."* Revelation says the land, or the earth, represents the land of Palestine.

What will be the purpose of the false prophet? Verse 12 explains, *"And he exerciseth all the power of the first beast before him, and causeth the earth and them which dwell therein to worship the first beast, whose deadly wound was healed."* The first beast mocks death and resurrection. Notice, I said "mocks" because Satan does not have the power of resurrection. He is going to fake death and fake resurrection because he realizes that in order to be the Messiah, he *must* have a death with a resurrection. Therefore, he must fake it. The false prophet will give testimony to him saying, "Hey, look! He has died, and now he is resurrected!"

Verse 14 states: *"And deceiveth them that dwell on the earth by the means of those miracles which he had power to do in the sight of the beast; saying to them that dwell on the earth, that they should make an image to the beast, which had the wound by a sword, and did live."* Men will be delivered by miracles. The false prophet will be a great orator. He will do miracles. He will speak great, lying wonders. He will fake death and resurrection. *"And he had power to give life unto the image of the beast, that the image of the beast should both speak, and cause that as many as would not worship the image of the beast should be killed"* (vs. 15).

Revelation 17:1 says: *"And there came one of the seven*

angels which had the seven vials, and talked with me, saying unto me, Come hither; I will shew unto thee the judgment of the great whore that sitteth upon many waters." You may ask, "What are those waters?" Let us now consider Revelation 17:15: *"And he saith unto me, The waters which thou sawest, where the whore sitteth, are peoples, and multitudes, and nations, and tongues."* In other words, it is a worldwide, false religious system. *"With whom the kings of the earth have committed fornication, and the inhabitants of the earth have been made drunk with the wine of her fornication"* (vs. 2).

Verse 3 states, *"So he carried me away in the spirit into the wilderness: and I saw a woman sit upon a scarlet coloured beast, full of names of blasphemy, having seven heads and ten horns."* Notice the similarity between the seven heads and ten horns--the symbols of religion and government.

The Mark

At that point and time, according to Daniel 7, the Antichrist will speak great and powerful things. He will do miracles. People will begin to say, "Well, I guess this has got to be the Messiah." He will change the laws. He will change the times and the seasons. Everything will be different.

In Daniel we read how life will be under Antichrist: *"And the ten horns out of this kingdom are ten kings that shall arise: and another shall rise after them; and he shall be diverse from the first, and he shall subdue three kings. And he shall speak great words against the most High, and shall wear out the saints of the most High, and think to change times and laws: and they shall be given into his hand until a time and times and the dividing of time. But the judgment shall sit, and they shall take away his dominion, to consume and to destroy it unto the end"* (Dan. 7:24-26).

Revelation 13:16-18 also explains: *"And he causeth all, both small and great, rich and poor, free and bond, to receive a* mark in their right hand, or in their foreheads: And that no man might buy or sell, save he that had the mark, or the name of the beast, or the number of his name. Here is wisdom. Let him that hath understanding count the number of the beast: for it is the number of a man; and his number is Six hundred threescore and six [or 666]." He will say, "Listen, if you are going to go to school, if you are going to buy food, if you are going to have a job, then you have to accept my mark."

I read an article written by a man who owns a company that designs small electronic devices--minuscule silicone chips. When a dog or cat is taken to the veterinarian for a vaccination, a chip is placed in the animal's back with a wand, thus allowing authorities to be able to prove exactly who the pet's owner is. This is done to cattle in Canada, also. Incredibly, leading companies are now considering how soon these same chips can be implanted into people who perform various jobs functions. Cosmetically, the chip is concealed beneath the skin and is not noticeable. However, it does not escape the scanners that register all movement of those who go in and out of those areas being monitored. What a great way to "brand" people.

You know what? If you don't take the mark of the Antichrist (whether it is a chip or not, I don't know), you will not be able to buy or sell. You will not be able to hold a job or buy food at the grocery store. The Antichrist will require that everyone commit to him. I believe there is a coming mark, but only after the Rapture of the church.

Right On Schedule

When Christ returns, He will defeat Antichrist and his cohorts. "These shall make war with the Lamb, and the Lamb shall overcome them: for he is Lord of lords, and King of kings: and they that are with him are called, and chosen, and faithful" (Rev. 17:14).

Is the lamb a pretty good fighter? Not usually. This Lamb, however, is going to fight the beast, and the Lamb is going to win. I believe the Lamb is none other than the Lamb of God, the person of Calvary, Jesus Christ. You see, history has recorded it. Reading on in Daniel 7:13-14, we find these words: "*I saw in the night visions, and, behold, one like the Son of man came with the clouds of heaven, and came to the Ancient of days, and they brought him near before him. And there was given him dominion, and glory, and a kingdom, that all people, nations, and languages, should serve him: his dominion is an everlasting dominion, which shall not pass away, and his kingdom that which shall not be destroyed.*"

Yes, friend, everything is right on schedule. Didn't the Bible say that Israel would be back in the land? Iraq would be destroyed once, twice, then devastated the last time? Is Germany reunited? Is Israel not reborn? Is Europe reconfiguring into a New Order, the Roman Empire reviving?

My dear friend, I believe we are living in the last days. No other generation who ever lived on planet earth has seen as much as you and I have seen. Subsequently, no other people who have ever lived are as accountable as we are. You and I are responsible for deciding whether we will spend eternity in heaven with Jesus Christ who died and rose again to save us, or whether we will spend an eternity in hell with Satan and his demonic fallen angels, for whom hell was created in order that sin can ultimately be purged and God's creation reconciled to Himself.

Jesus is the Prince of Life. Satan is the cannibal of death. You decide. Jesus is the truth and the life. Satan is the father of lies and the master of death. You decide.

Where Will You Spend Eternity?

The story is told of a man who once had a stray dog show

up on his porch. For a day or two, he tolerated the dog, then he decided he had to get rid of the critter. But, the dog was faithful, and it followed him everywhere, no matter where he went or what he did. Frustrated by this faithful old dog, the man said, "I have got to get rid of this dog."

He didn't have the heart to shoot the dog, so he loaded him into a simple row boat along with a big brick and rope. When he reached the middle of the lake, he called the faithful dog over to him, tied the rope around its neck, and the other end around the brick. Then he threw dog, brick, and rope into the lake. But the brick was not heavy enough to pull the dog all the way under!

Still being faithful, the old dog swam around and around and around the boat trying to get back to his master, all the while hauling the brick around with him. Now frustrated, the man felt he had to drown the dog somehow. He took an oar and began to hit the dog on the head, trying to poke it under the water. In the course of doing this, the man fell overboard into the lake, and he could not swim.

Seeing the man thrashing in the water himself, the dog came over, grabbed him by the collar, and began to swim toward the shore towing the brick, rope, and man. Finally, when the dog could swim no longer, the man put his feet down, only to find that he could now walk up on the bank. He looked back to find the brick had finally taken its toll on the dog--he had drowned.

When I heard this story, it made me think about a tale even more pathetic. I think an old man who would drown a dog is a pretty cruel man. But, I will tell you what is more cruel--for a person not to receive Christ! Jesus came to earth and did nothing but good. But some people don't want Him; they do everything they can to get rid of Him and keep Him out of their lives. They don't realize that the gospel is a story of love and faithfulness: *"For God so loved the world, that he gave his only begotten Son..."* (John 3:16). He sent His Son to die for you.

I don't know your heart's condition, but I do know that Jesus paid an incredible price to save you. He gave His life, and He did it willingly. If you have never received Christ as your personal Savior, then you need to make that decision today.

Jesus allows you the option to say, "No, I don't want to be saved." He died for you; He arose again. The gospel is available, but He lets you say no--the choice is yours.

Do you know what keeps a person from coming to Christ once they know they need Him? It is something called pride. Jesus Himself said, *"No man comes to the Father [God] but by me."* To be saved, simply admit to God that you are a sinner.

Dear friend, Christ came to this wretched, strife-torn, sinful world to save sinners. To qualify for the gospel of Jesus Christ, you have to be a sinner. And, you are a sinner whether you admit it or not. But, if you'll admit it, if you come to Christ who loves you so much He died for you, He will save you in an instant.

Instead of going through eternity in hell, where you and I deserve to go, you will live eternally in heaven, where God has a place reserved for you. Because of the sacrifice the Lord Jesus Christ made for you and me on that cruel Roman cross nearly 2,000 years ago, you can live forever. Accept Him today. He is the only way.

Marriage Supper or Tribulation?

Most of us have witnessed the end of a basketball game and have seen that as the people come out, some are happy and smiling; others look like they have just received a speeding ticket. What is the difference? Well, one team won, and the other lost. In this chapter we are going to look at a seven-year period in which one "team" will lose, and the other will win. On the earth it will be called the Tribulation; but if we know Christ as our Savior, we will be in heaven celebrating the Marriage Supper of the Lamb. This seven-year period will be preceded by the Rapture of the church and followed by the Battle of Armageddon and the revealing of Christ for who He is. In this chapter we will be looking at these very important, significant events that could well begin anytime--whenever Christ returns.

As we look at the Tribulation and the Marriage Supper, we will view them against an important background that has been woven throughout the first six chapters. Our theme verse states a basic truth from which to consider these events. *"We have also a more sure word of prophecy; whereunto ye do well that ye take heed, as unto a light that shineth in a dark place, until the day dawn, and the day star arise* [until Christ comes]*in your hearts"* (2 Pet. 1:19).

Although we will be looking at future events, we know we have a more sure Word of prophecy. We have also learned that the Bible says every promise of God is "yes," and in Him guaranteed. So as we look at the prophecy concerning the Marriage Supper, we know God has promised to fulfill every detail of it. We have already clearly determined the accuracy of Bible prophecy. God will keep His promises!

We have looked at many things to determine that this is the day and the time when we can reasonably say Christ could come back. I like what someone said after studying Bible prophecies: "I used to think that it was possible for Christ to come back in my lifetime; but after studying this subject, I have decided that it is probable that Christ will come back in my lifetime." Are you really ready if Christ were to come today? Is there even a shadow of a doubt in your mind where you stand with Christ? The promises of God are made to give us assurance that when He comes we will be ready.

We have seen prophecy after prophecy fulfilled, including the rebirth of Israel and the rise of Russia. We have read in Daniel that in the days just before Christ comes there will be a great increase in technology; and, in our time, we have seen organ and heart transplants become almost common-place occurrences. We have seen great advances in communication and transportation as well. We have also learned that in the last days, exactly as the Bible says, the powers of the world will look to the Middle East because there will be something of tremendous value--oil. We have witnessed the OPEC nations making $200 billion profit in one year by selling oil. This is twice the combined profit of all the corporations in the United States for the same period of time! We have looked at the incredible story of the ashes of the red heifer and we have seen how the people of Israel, including the conservative orthodox Jews, are looking for Messiah to come.

Oh, what a fortunate people we are! But we are also

accountable, for we live in America where current news reports and the Word of God are easily available. I believe that as we stand before God in a coming day, every American who really knows Christ as Savior will be called upon to give an account for the fact that we held in our hands the Word of God. What have we done with what we have? I think we should be preparing now for the coming of Christ.

One thing I want to emphasize is that it is impossible for a person to be neutral concerning the second coming of Christ. It is not a subject where one can say, "Well, it really doesn't matter what you believe." I believe as we study God's Word, we see that every writer of a New Testament epistle had a very strong view about His return: Christ was coming back. It motivated and changed the life of every writer of a New Testament book. Should it do any less for us living 1,900 years later? I think the impact upon us should be tremendous.

Christ Will Return: The Rapture of the Church

The Bible states in Acts 1:10-11 that Christ ascended into heaven. The disciples who were on the Mount of Olives looked up as Christ went into heaven, and two men in white apparel said, "...*Ye men of Galilee, why stand ye gazing up into heaven? this same Jesus, which is taken up from you into heaven, shall so come in like manner* [the same way] *as ye have seen him go into heaven.*"

We need to realize that He went bodily into heaven. This means that He will bodily come back to the earth. There are some people who say, "He will not really come back bodily to the earth, just the Spirit of God will come back." Nothing could be further from the truth! This would be an absolute violation of Acts 1:10! I also believe that He will come right back to the Mount of Olives when He returns to set His feet upon the earth. The Old Testament is clear about this in Zechariah 14:4. But also note that the bodily return of Christ to the Mount of Olives is after the Tribulation period. Before the Tribulation, however, Christ will come back for the church. This coming for the church is called the Rapture. I Thessalonians 4:17 says this meeting will take place in the clouds instead of on the earth.

In Acts 2, on the Day of Pentecost, the Spirit of God came down and the church age began. The period of time from A.D. 32 (the Day of Pentecost) until the Lord comes back is referred to as the church age. The Bible tells us that this age will end with the sound of a trumpet, the voice of an archangel, and the invitation, "Come up here!" Everyone who has received Christ will be gone in an instant of time. The church, the people who are saved and still on the earth, will be raptured.

Now one of my favorite things is for people who do not believe in the second coming of Christ to say to me, "The word *rapture* isn't in the Bible." They are right; it is not there. But the phrase "snatch out" is there, to "catch away" is there. The Latin word to describe the phrase "catch out" is the word *rapito*, or our English word *rapture*.

By the way, do you know that the word *Bible* is not in the Bible? But I still believe that it is the Word of God, don't you? The word *Trinity* is not in the Bible, but I still believe in the Trinity, don't you? Just because the particular word *rapture* is not there, it will not keep the church from being snatched out or raptured.

The first aspect of the return of Christ is that He will come for the church. He will come for His bride. (In the Bible the church is referred to as the bride of Christ.) The second phase is at the end of the seven-year Tribulation period when He will come back **with** His bride. So He comes first **for** His bride (Rapture), and then He will come **with** His bride.

After the church is Raptured, the first thing to occur will be the Judgment Seat of Christ. This is a time when every believer individually will stand before Christ and give account of his life from the day he received Christ until his rapture, or until he was taken by death. I really believe that God will investigate every thought, every motive, and every deed. He will replay our thoughts. Now I do not know what that does to you, but I know what that does to me. There are some things that I have thought that I would rather you not know, but I would not be as embarrassed about you knowing as I would about the Lord knowing and reviewing those matters.

That is the advantage of 1 John 1:9: *"If we confess our sins, he is faithful and just to forgive us our sins."* So as I am watching the videotape of my thought life, my deeds, and my motives, every once in a while there will be a blank scene on the screen. That's when He forgave me! Isn't that going to be wonderful! Listen, the purpose of God at the Judgment Seat of Christ is to hand out rewards, but it is possible to lose them. It is possible to be disqualified--not from salvation--but from rewards. After the Judgment Seat of Christ, we will go to the Marriage Supper of the Lamb. What a delightful time that will be!

That will be the scene in heaven. But at the same time the believers are going to the Judgment Seat of Christ and the Marriage Supper of the Lamb, there will be another judgment on earth--the judgment of the Jews on the earth during the Tribulation period. It will be the most dreadful period of time that the earth has ever known. People will cry out for the mountains to fall on them. That is how awful it will be. There is only one way to be sure that we will be delivered from that seven-year period--receive Christ as Savior. If for no other reason, I would receive Christ as Savior just to be gone before the seven-year period. Anyone who knows Christ can rest assured that he will not go through the Tribulation.

During this time of Tribulation, wars will take place. Among them will be the invasion by Russia into Israel. A second war is called the War in Heaven. The third war will occur at the end of the Tribulation and is called the Battle of Armageddon. Then there will be a final war at the end of the Millennial reign. These are the four wars that the Bible indicates are yet to come.

In this chapter, we are going to be looking primarily at the time between the Rapture and the Battle of Armageddon. John 13:36-38 states: *"Simon Peter said unto him, Lord, whither goest thou? Jesus answered him, Whither I go, thou canst not follow me now; but thou shalt follow me afterwards. Peter said unto him, Lord, why cannot I follow thee now? I will lay down my life for thy sake. Jesus answered him, Wilt thou lay down your life for my sake? Verily, verily, I say unto thee, The cock shall not crow, till thou hast denied me thrice."*

Christ said to the disciples, "Listen, I am getting ready to go somewhere and where I am going, you can't come." Peter and the rest of the disciples said, "Wait a minute! We have given up our jobs to follow You. We'll go. If You're just thinking that we are afraid of the Jews that have been threatening You, don't worry, we'll go with You. As long as we are with You, we are not afraid." Peter continued by saying, "Listen, I don't care, even if I have to go with You unto death, I'll go!" That was a brave statement, wasn't it? I really believe that the Lord Jesus was talking about something far beyond what Peter could imagine, and this distressed Peter.

Christ continued as He saw in Peter's eyes that his heart was troubled: *"Let not your heart be troubled: ye believe in God, believe also in me"* (John 14:1). That is wonderful to know! Do you know that Christ gave us information about His second coming so that our hearts would not be troubled?*"In my*

Father's house are many mansions [dwelling places]: *if it were not so, I would have told you. I go to prepare a place for you. And if I go and prepare a place for you, I will come again, and receive you unto myself; that where I am, there ye may be also. And whither I go ye know, and the way ye know. Thomas saith unto him, Lord, we know not whither thou goest; and how can we know the way? Jesus saith unto him, I am the way, the truth, and the life: no man cometh unto the Father, but by me*" (vss. 2-6).

That is a wonderful portion of scripture! I believe that as He said those words, He was only a few short hours away from the cross. The promise that He made to those disciples was an incredible one. He said, "Don't you know that in My Father's house there are many dwelling places." Never get the idea that in heaven there will be a whole neighborhood of mansions and that each of us will have a great, big house. There is **one** house, and that is God's. In that one mansion, all of us will dwell together with Christ.

One thrilling part of this is that He said, "The reason I'm going away is so I can prepare it for **you**." Now, I really believe that creation, as we see it right now, was created by Him in less than one week. As a matter of fact, He even took one entire day off to rest. But I want to remind you that He has been in heaven preparing a place for us for 1,900 years. Don't you think that is going to be special? I do. Since He created the world in six days, can you imagine what our heavenly dwelling place is going to be like after He's spent 1,900 years preparing! I believe He is almost finished, and the minute it is ready He is going to call us. One reason I believe this is because of the wonderful parallel between the Jewish wedding and the snatching out of Christ's bride. Let's look at some of the details of a Jewish wedding ceremony and the preparations for it.

The Wedding Ceremony: The Bride of Christ

I am not sure that those of us who live in a modern western civilization understand all the Bible says concerning the catching out of a bride. Remember this Word was given to the people in terms of a Jewish setting since Jewish people were the ones hearing the Word. We need to understand the Jewish wedding in order to know what God is saying to us.

The first major step toward a Jewish wedding is called a betrothal. In this betrothal period, the bridegroom takes the initiative and finds a bride that he desires, and travels from his house to the bride's home. There he makes a bargain with the father of the bride, and they agree upon a price. After the groom pays the price, he seals the bargain: he makes a covenant relationship. This is done by pouring a cup of wine; and, with the drinking of that cup of wine, the groom states, "The bargain is sealed. The price is paid. She belongs to me." Then the groom leaves and goes back to his father's house alone.

Right next to his father's house, and sometimes even in his father's house, the groom begins to build a place where he and his bride can live. As soon as he is through building that dwelling place in his father's house, he goes back for his bride. But the bride does not know when he will come. Normally, it is at night, but she does not know when it will be. All she knows is that she is to be ready. She is to have her dress ready; she is to have the whole bridal party ready so that at a moment's notice when he comes back and calls, "Are you ready?" she can quickly gather her things and rush out to meet him. Then they depart to the father's house.

That is the signal to the family and friends of the couple that seven days later there will be a great wedding ceremony. At the end of those seven days, they are to come to the celebration. In the meantime, the bride and bridegroom are in the father's house, and together they seal the bond of marriage. For the first time, they have a physical union; and, in the privacy of the father's house, they spend those seven days together. At the end of those seven days, the groom comes out and introduces his bride to all the guests that have come for the celebration.

There are some wonderful parallels between the Jewish wedding ceremony and Christ with His bride. First of all, in Ephesians 5:22-33, you will find that Christ says that the church is a bride; not like a bride, but it **is** a bride. All the way through the Bible we find that Christ desires a bride. If you are single, you may be quite anxious to get married and can relate to that desire. But just remember that Christ has waited 1,900 years for His bride. He has been so patient, but I believe He is now anxiously awaiting the moment when He can come back and claim His bride.

As we continue to look at these amazing parallels, we are reminded that there was a time when Christ left His Father's home (heaven) and made a trip all the way to earth. The price that was asked for the bride (the church) was His own precious blood, and Christ was willing to pay the price. He went to the cross. He died. If there had been any way to secure salvation other than by dying, He would have paid it, for nothing could be more precious than the life of the Lord Jesus. He loved His bride so much that He was willing to pay that tremendous price.

I also want us to remember that on the night that He was betrayed, He took the cup and, with His disciples, He said, *"This is the covenant of my blood; it is given for you."* It may only be a symbol to us, but it was a covenant, a promise. He drank that cup to seal the bargain and to show that He was willing to pay the price of giving His life to redeem His bride.

Then, just as in the case of a Jewish wedding, He left

earth and returned to His Father's house in heaven to prepare a home for His bride. The Bible says that in the coming day He is going to come back just like the Jewish groom returns. In the meantime, just like the Jewish bride is making herself ready, the bride of Christ is to be getting herself ready so that when the shout is given, "Come up here!" she will be ready to go. I believe the Bible is clear that the church will be caught up together with Him and go to the Judgment Seat of Christ and the Marriage Supper of the Lamb.

At the end of seven years He will come back with the church, His bride, and will introduce her to all the world. For the first time, she will be unveiled. Do you see the beautiful parallel between this introduction at the end of the Tribulation and when the Jewish groom introduces his bride to the wedding party at the end of seven days? This parallel of the Jewish wedding with Christ and the church is so exact, so clear; I don't think anyone can miss it! We can be sure that Christ will return for His bride.

The Rapture of the Church: A Message of Comfort

1 Thessalonians 4:13 addresses the concern of what happens to those believers who die before the Rapture: "*But I would not have you to be ignorant, brethren, concerning them which are asleep* [those who have died], *that ye sorrow not, even as others which have no hope.*"

Those at Thessalonica had only enjoyed the ministry of Paul for a month. During the course of that time, they had touched on a number of subjects, among which was the second coming of Christ. Some of the people were concerned because they thought that those who had already died would miss the second coming of Christ. Paul wrote back to them and proclaimed, "I want you to know that those who have died have not missed anything." "*For if we believe that Jesus died and rose again, even so them also which sleep in Jesus will God bring with Him. For this we say unto you by the word of the Lord, that we which are alive and remain* [Paul really believed he would be alive when Christ returned] *unto the coming of the Lord shall not prevent* [precede] *them which are asleep. For the Lord himself shall descend from heaven with a shout, with the voice of the archangel, and with the trump of God: and the dead in Christ shall rise first* "(vss. 14-16).

The first thing that will happen as Christ returns is that those who have already died will receive their glorified bodies as they go to meet Christ in the air. Verse 17 describes what will happen to those believers who are still alive on the earth: "*Then we which are alive and remain shall be caught up together with them in the clouds, to meet the Lord in the air: and so shall we ever be with the Lord.*"

The words "caught up" could be translated "snatched away," or "raptured." "*Wherefore comfort one another with these words*" (vs. 18).

Knowing what will take place was meant to be a great comfort, but this was only the beginning of what he said will happen to the church, the people who believe in Christ. Look at 1 Corinthians 15:51-52: "*Behold, I shew you a mystery; We shall not all sleep, but we shall all be changed, In a moment, in the twinkling of an eye, at the last trump: for the trumpet shall sound, and the dead shall be raised incorruptible, and we shall be changed.*"

So the custom of the Jewish bridegroom was not to send a message saying, "I'm going to be there two days from now." Rather, the bride was to be so prepared that whenever he came, she would be ready. We see that at any moment, with no announcement, Christ can come and call us out to go to the Marriage Supper of the Lamb! It will be vastly different for those who are not a part of the bride of Christ (the church), for those are the ones who will go through the Tribulation.

The Time of Tribulation

It is important to notice that for the church, there will be no specific signs given concerning the second coming of Christ. All the signs are for the Tribulation. This is a fact that is worth repeating: every sign is a warning for the Tribulation. There is no sign for the church. Believers are to be so much in love with Christ that we will be ready at any time for the coming of Christ. The signs are given to an evil and adulterous generation, not to the church. If we are looking for signs, we won't find any, for the signs that are given point to the Tribulation, and the church will be gone before it begins. So as we see these things coming to pass--these signs of the Tribulation--we should know that it means the coming of Christ is that much nearer.

What is the sequence of events? First of all, there is the catching away of the church, a secret snatching away. He comes, gives a shout, and everyone who has received Christ will be gone in an instant. I believe in that instant of time, there will be a great fear in the hearts of every man and woman remaining on the earth. I also believe the following Sunday after the Rapture occurs, every church building in the world will be filled to capacity. I don't think there will be an available copy of the Bible anywhere; it will be that much in demand. I believe it will become a "best-seller," and people will read it. I am convinced that in the hearts and the minds of people, there will be a great fear and a great sense of emptiness. The Bible says that in that day there will be such a loneliness and longing of people for God. They will cry out to God, but there will be no answer. This is the awful tragedy. Today is the day and the age of grace. The Spirit of God beckons to people, begs people, to receive Him now before it is too late.

To see what happens next, look at 2 Thessalonians 2:1- 2: "*Now we beseech you, brethren, by the coming of our Lord Jesus Christ, and by our gathering together unto him* [there's the Rapture--the Rapture is a gathering together unto Him], *that ye be not soon shaken in mind, or be troubled, neither by spirit, nor by word, nor by letter as from us, as that the day of Christ is at hand.*"

Paul said, "We are living right in the day and the time when Christ could come." And there is someone else who is coming. "*Let no man deceive you by any means: for that day shall not come, except there come a falling away first, and that man of sin be revealed, the son of perdition; Who opposeth and exalteth himself above all that is called God, or that is worshipped; so that he as God sitteth in the temple of God, shewing himself that he is God. Remember ye not, that, when I was yet with you, I told you these things?*" (vss. 3-5).

Remember, this is Paul's second letter to these people; he had warned them about the Antichrist before. He says, "Didn't I tell you about these things?" He told them in I Thessalonians, and he told them when he was there in person. "*And now ye know what withholdeth that he might be revealed in his time*" (vs. 6).

There is something that prevents the Antichrist from coming. "*For the mystery of iniquity doth already work: only he who now letteth will let* [hinders, will continue to hinder], *until he be taken out of the way*" (vs. 7). When the Spirit of God is taken out of the way, then the Antichrist will be free to come in and rule the hearts and minds of men.

Let me remind you that Satan is a liar. He is a master at deception. He went to Eve in the Garden, and was so appealing and so subtle in his way, that Eve, who knew something of the presence of God and who had heard the voice of God, believed the lie of Satan. Do not think for one minute, if you have not received Christ in this present day and age of grace, that in the time of Tribulation you will receive Him! You will not! This is a lie of Satan, one of his worst! When the one that hinders the Antichrist, the Spirit of God, is taken out with the church, then the Antichrist can work. *"And then shall that Wicked be revealed, whom the Lord shall consume with the spirit of his mouth, and shall destroy with the brightness of his coming: Even him, whose coming is after the working of Satan with all power and signs and lying wonders"* (vss. 8-9).

Today the world requires signs. The Antichrist will come and give more signs than anyone could ever imagine. I believe that he will heal people and raise people from the dead, and people will say, "He must be Christ! He is doing exactly what the Bible says Christ did!" People will watch him on television as he performs these things and as he makes persuasive personal appearances. *"And with all deceiveableness of unrighteousness in them that perish; because they received not the love of the truth, that they might be saved"* (vs. 10).

See the people that are deceived? Those that receive not the love of the truth, those that heard that Christ died and rose again and did not receive Him; they will be blinded and deceived by the Antichrist. *"And for this cause God shall send them strong delusion, that they should believe a lie: That they all might be damned [judged] who believed not the truth, but had pleasure in unrighteousness "*(vss. 11-12).

If there is a passage in the Bible that is frightening, it is this one. I believe that people in America who have heard the gospel and have had such access to it, and still do not receive Christ, will be among those who will be lost forever. They will go through the Tribulation; they will literally be duped by the Antichrist.

You cannot be neutral in that day because you will either receive Christ or you will receive the Antichrist. Those are the only two choices. There will be no such thing as an agnostic, or an atheist, or a neutral person in that day.

The Marriage Supper of the Lamb

John says in Revelation 18:20, *"Rejoice over her, thou heaven, and ye holy apostles and prophets; for God hath avenged you on her."* He is saying, "Rejoice over the false church, because it has been done in." And then in Revelation 19:7, the Marriage Supper of the Lamb is described: *"Let us be glad and rejoice, and give honour to him: for the marriage of the Lamb is come, and his wife hath made herself ready."* That is going to be a great day! *"And to her was granted that she should be arrayed in fine linen, clean and white: for the fine linen is the righteousness of saints. And he saith unto me, Write, Blessed are they which are called unto the marriage supper of the Lamb. And he saith unto me, These are the true sayings of God. And I fell at his feet to worship him. And he said unto me, See thou do it not: I am thy fellow-servant, and of thy brethren that have the testimony of Jesus: worship God: for the testimony of Jesus is the spirit of prophecy"* (vss. 8-10).

This celebration will be a great day for every Christian. At the end of the Marriage Supper of the Lamb, at the end of this great celebration, Christ says to the church, "I love you so much. I am so pleased with My bride because you are spotless and dressed in white. You are wonderful to Me. I want to tell you what will happen."

Then in verse 11 we read, *"And I saw heaven opened...."* Now, the last time heaven opened was in Revelation 4:1, when a shout was given and an invitation was made that said, "Come up here," and the church was Raptured. The church is in heaven from Revelation 4 all the way to Revelation 19:11. This is the time frame of the Marriage Supper of the Lamb in heaven, and the Tribulation on earth. Can you imagine what it is going to be like to be on a seven-year honeymoon in heaven? Often people say, "Will we know what is going on in the Tribulation?" Well, you can look if you want to, but I am going to be on my honeymoon, and I am not sure that I will have time to check on what's going on below. For seven years, seven wonderful years, we will be in the presence of Christ.

During those same seven years, it will be like hell on earth. The Bible describes this dreadful time. *"And I saw heaven opened and, behold a white horse; and he that sat upon him was called Faithful and True* [this has to be Christ], *and in righteousness he doth judge and make war. His eyes were as a flame of fire, and on his head were many crowns; and he had a name written, that no man knew, but he himself. And he was clothed with a vesture dipped in blood: and his name is called The Word of God.* [Who is this? It has to be Christ.] *And the armies which were in heaven followed him upon white horses, clothed in fine linen, white and clean"* (vss. 11-14).

Who do you think this is that's wearing fine linen and riding on white horses? It is His bride. Isn't that going to be wonderful? I am going to know how to ride a horse in that day!

By the way, the church does not do any fighting. Would you dress someone up in white, fine linen to fight? No, we will just be cheerleaders. Christ will do the fighting! *And out of his mouth goeth a sharp sword, that with it he should smite the nations: and he shall rule them with a rod of iron: and he treadeth the winepress of the fierceness and wrath of Almighty God. And he hath on his vesture and on his thigh a name written, KING OF KINGS, AND LORD OF LORDS"* (vss. 15-16).

The description that follows in verses 17-21 talks of something called Armageddon. When Christ comes back with the church at the end of the Tribulation, Armageddon will take place. Armageddon is a supper. Although it is not the Marriage Supper of the Lamb, it is a supper. The menu is given in verse 18: *That ye may eat the flesh of kings, and the flesh of captains, and the flesh of mighty men, and the flesh of horses, and of them that sit on them, and the flesh of all men, both free and bond, both small and great.*"

I am sure I do not want to attend that supper! John tells us that after the church goes to heaven to be with Christ, the earth will go through the most terrible time. At the end of that time, Christ will come back with the church, and the Battle of Armageddon will be fought. All the nations will come against Israel, and Christ will come back. The Bible says that with the brightness of His coming (Matt. 24-25), He will destroy those nations.

Then what follows is a thousand-year period called a Millennial Reign when Christ will rule the earth. That's when the child will play with the snake, and the lamb and the lion will lie down next to one another. A baby will live to be 100 years old, and other people will live to be 1,000 years old. It will be an incredible time!

We cannot be sure exactly when this will occur, but I want to point out an interesting parallel. There were six days of creation, and on the seventh day God rested. Now parallel the six days of creation with the 6,000 years of Adam to the end of the Tribulation (4,000 years from Adam to Christ, 2,000 years from Christ until the end of the Tribulation). Then compare the seventh day to the 7,000th year. It would be interesting if that is the time of the Millennium, the time of rest. This is a perfect parallel of God's creation of the earth and His ultimate plan for the earth.

God Has a Plan for You

God has a plan for our lives. He has a perfect plan for

you. If you will come to Him, and believe that Christ died for you and that He arose again, you can become a part of His grand plan for your life. His plan is for you to be a part of the bride of Christ and for you to join Him at the Marriage Supper of the Lamb. This is His desire for every person. We read in 1 John 4:14: "*And we have seen and do testify that the Father sent the Son to be the Savior of the world.*"

Have you accepted Him as your Savior? Are you prepared to join Him at the Marriage Supper of the Lamb? This is the day and age of grace, and it could end at any moment with His return. Don't believe Satan's lie that there will still be time later to accept Christ; don't be deceived.

Christ has a grand and glorious plan for His bride, His church. Will you come and be a part of that plan? Are you ready to join Him at the Marriage Supper? It's either the Marriage Supper or the Tribulation; there is no neutral ground.

Details of the Tribulation

I want to take some time to look more closely at some specific aspects of the Tribulation from Revelation 6. This chapter corresponds to the time referred to in 2 Thessalonians 2 where Paul says, "*After the Spirit of God is removed, now the antichrist is revealed.*"

Remember, however, that the Rapture of the church does not begin the Tribulation. The thing that begins the Tribulation (Dan. 9:27) is the Antichrist signing a peace treaty with Israel. How long it is between the Rapture of the church and the treaty signing is not known. It could occur simultaneously. It could be one day later, or one month, or one year. Chances are, it will occur soon afterward, but we are not told that the Rapture begins the Tribulation. We are told that the signing of the peace treaty actually begins the Tribulation.

Revelation 5 shows us that there will be a book sealed with seven seals. Other parts of Revelation reveal that there will be seven trumpets and seven bowls. There is a progression of one to another like a telescope. The seven seals will be opened; and, in the seventh seal, seven trumpets will come out. In the seventh trumpet, seven bowls will come out. "*And I saw when the Lamb opened one of the seals, and I heard, as it were the noise of thunder, one of the four beasts saying, Come and see*" (Rev. 6:1).

As He opens the first seal of this book, out comes one to the four corners of the earth. "*And I saw, and behold a white horse: and he that sat on him had a bow; and a crown was given unto him: and he went forth conquering, and to conquer*" (vs. 2). It's not Christ; it's the Antichrist that is going forth to conquer here!

"*And when he had opened the second seal, I heard the second beast say, Come and see. And there went out another horse that was red: and power was given to him that sat thereon to take peace from the earth, and that they should kill one another: and there was given unto him a great sword* "(vss. 3-4). Remember from our study concerning Russia that in the midst of a time when they are talking peace, Israel will set down every weapon. Israel has the fourth largest army in the world, but they will set down their arms because they will have signed a peace treaty. When they say "peace," the Antichrist will come unto them with a great sword, and war will begin. If we do a little death tally in the book of Revelation, we find that less than half of the people on the face of the earth will still be alive seven years later. That's how dreadful it will be.

"*And when he had opened the third seal, I heard the third beast say, Come and see. And I beheld, and lo a black horse; and he that sat on him had a pair of balances in his hand. And I heard a voice in the midst of the four beasts say, A measure of wheat for a penny, and three measures of barley for a penny; and see thou hurt not the oil and the wine. And when he had opened the fourth seal...and behold a pale horse: and his name that sat on him was Death*" (vss. 5-8). A study of Revelation reveals that he will come to kill a fourth part of the earth. There will be famine, and one-fourth of the population of the world will die of starvation.

I know the United Nations does not believe that the book of Revelation can be taken literally, but I want you to know that recently as the World Food Bank did their calculations, they estimated that by the end of this decade one-half billion people will have starved to death. That will be one-fourth of the world, which is exactly the number that John penned 1,900 years ago. They could have saved the several million dollars it took to do the study if only they had read Revelation!

The fifth seal will be a seal of martyrdom (vss. 9-11). The sixth seal will be treason and anarchy (vss. 12-17). As these seals are brought forth, tremendous judgment comes out. I want us to notice verses 15-17: "*And the kings of the earth, and the great men, and the rich men, and the chief captains, and the mighty men, and every bondman [slave], and every free man, hid themselves in the dens and in the rocks of the mountains; And said to the mountains and rocks, Fall on us, and hide us from the face of him that sitteth on the throne, and from the wrath of the Lamb: For the great day of his wrath is come; and who shall be able to stand?*"

It is not necessary for a single person that is alive today to remain on planet earth at that time. No one will be there unless they choose to be, and the way you choose to be there is to say, "I am neutral to Christ." You do not have to be opposed to Him, just be neutral to Him. Where do you stand? You are either saved and on your way to heaven, or you will go through one of the most horrible times ever. In Revelation 7:9-10 we read that there will be multitudes saved: *"After this I beheld, and, lo, a great multitude, which no man could number, of all nations, and kindreds, and people, and tongues, stood before the throne, and before the Lamb, clothed with white robes, and palms in their hands; And cried with a loud voice, saying, Salvation to our God which sitteth upon the throne, and unto the Lamb."*

This passage declares those who will be saved during the Tribulation, but they are **only** people who have never heard or refused the gospel in the day and age of grace. And they will become martyrs for their newfound faith in Christ. They will be killed by the Antichrist.

What about those who have heard or refused Him prior to the Tribulation and the Rapture of the church? Think of it this way. Why would people who have already heard and have refused Him during a time when there was no penalty or punishment, come to Him when they would immediately be killed for their acceptance of Christ? I do not think they will come to Him when it will cost them their lives. People's outright refusal to accept Christ, plus the lie of Satan to deceive people into believing the Antichrist, will cause many to be hopelessly lost. We find indications of this in 2 Thessalonians 2:10-12 and Matthew 25:1-13. Now is the day and age of grace; now is the time to receive Christ. Have you received Him?

The Horrors of the Tribulation and the Atomic Age

I want us to concentrate on another aspect of the Tribulation found in Revelation 8. At this time He will open the seventh seal. *"And when he had opened the seventh seal, there was silence in heaven about the space of half an hour"* (vs. 1).

This judgment is going to be so terrible that heaven will be silent. As the trumpets begin to come out of the seventh seal, tremendous things happen. First of all in verse 7, notice that as the trumpet is sounded, hail comes mixed with fire and blood. As it comes to the earth, a third of all the trees will be burnt up, and all the green grass will be destroyed. Many people think this will occur in the United States because North America makes up a third of all the earth's land mass. It could be.

Most Bible commentators 100 years ago wondered what could be so devastating that a third of all the earth would be burnt up instantly. Well, now we know. We live in what is called the "Atomic Age." It is an amazing age, and I think it is important to understand more about it.

When did the atomic age come about? In January of 1939, a German scientist succeeded in splitting the atom. In 1942, December 2 at 3:36 p.m., the world entered the atomic age. Scientists at the University of Chicago produced the first continually controlled chain reaction fission process. They expected that some day great power would be obtained, and that we would be amazed at its usefulness.

Scientists developed an atomic bomb between December 2, 1942, and July 16, 1945. At 5:20 a.m. on that July day they set it off in the desert of New Mexico. They built a tower 70 feet tall out of 10-inch rail, and each foot of rail weighed 90 pounds. When they set off the bomb, the tower exploded and was tossed seven miles into the air, vaporized as it went up. The bomb blew a hole in the ground 60 feet deep and 5,000 feet wide. For 18,000 feet in all directions it boiled, it fused, it melted the sand together so that it was a sea of glass.

The astonished scientists said, "It had more power than we imagined!" They were so proud of it that they dropped the next bomb just a month later, on August 6, 1945. That bomb was 14 feet long, 5 feet in diameter, and weighed 10,000 pounds. It was dropped on Hiroshima. The results of that clumsy bomb dropped from 18,000 feet affected 350,000 people, 70,000 of which died instantly. Two-thirds of the buildings in a huge radius were destroyed immediately. Many hundreds of thousands were affected for life because of radiation. Three days later, 47 other cities were sent leaflets warning them a similar destruction would come. Another bomb was dropped on one other city, Nagasaki.

Russia exploded its first atomic bomb in August 1949. We in the U.S. decided that if the Russians had the atomic bomb, we should develop something more significant. We developed the hydrogen bomb a few years later. Instead of a fission process, it is a fusion process which burns at a temperature of 20,000 degrees Fahrenheit, roughly the temperature of the sun's surface.

On November 1, 1951, in the Pacific Ocean, we tested the first hydrogen bomb. We bombed a one-mile island and literally blew it out of the ocean. A bomb also blew a hole in the ocean floor 175 feet deep. The second bomb exploded in 1954 was even more powerful than the first. It was light enough that it could be carried in a small passenger airplane. Do you see the progress we were making? It is believed that the radiation from one bomb could affect every living person on planet earth.

I want you to know that the atom and hydrogen bombs are out of date. We now have developed the neutron bomb. It is even more powerful and devastating! In the Tribulation period of time, although there will not be total destruction to the earth, I believe there will be nuclear blasts that will affect major portions of it. Let's look at 2 Peter 3:10-11: "*But the day of the Lord will come as a thief in the night; in the which the heavens shall pass away with a great noise, and the elements shall melt with fervent heat, the earth also and the works that are therein shall be burned up. Seeing then that all these things shall be dissolved...."*

Although this total destruction will not take place until after the Tribulation is over, it appears that there will be something almost equal to it in the Tribulation. We can see some of what will happen in Revelation 8.

In Revelation 8:8-9, we see that the second trumpet sounds, and one-third of all the sea becomes blood, one-third of all the sea creatures die, and one-third of all the ships are destroyed. In verses 10-11, the third trumpet sounds, and a great star (I think this represents Satan) in heaven falls, and one-third of all the rivers are poisoned. In verses 12-13, we find the fourth trumpet, and one-third of all the planets are blasted out of the sky. In verse 13 we read, *"...Woe, woe, woe, to the inhabiters of the earth by reason of the other voices of the trumpet of the three angels, which are yet to sound!"* It is so bad that they are warned with three woes: "Oh, won't you repent!"

Then Revelation 9 tells us that even the daytime will be affected. The fifth trumpet will then sound and horrible creatures will be let loose from the pit of hell. These creatures will have great power and will go about the earth stinging and devouring men and women. People will cry out in tremendous pain. It says in verse 3 that the creatures will be like scorpions upon the earth having the face of men and hair like women. They will be straight out of the pit of hell!

Verse 16 of chapter 9 indicates that a great army will come from the east with 200 million men. Remember John wrote this when there were barely 200 million in the whole world. But today China could form this army, and they could march from the east. In the middle of the Tribulation (Rev. 12) God says, "Satan, I am going to restrict you to the earth."

When He does, Satan will become so enraged that he will bring great persecution upon Israel. We read in the Bible that one-fourth of the people will starve. One-third of all men will be burnt up. Five-sixths of the Russian army and the armies of the nations aligned with Russia will be destroyed. Two-thirds of Israel will be annihilated, and we have not even gotten into the Great Tribulation where death will reign.

Chapter 13 reveals that from this point on, just in order to have one morsel of food, everyone must brand themselves with the mark of the beast. It will be impossible to be neutral. Everyone who does not take the mark will be killed immediately.

In chapter 14:20, a valley is described. It will be 180 miles long, and it will be filled with blood up to the bridles of horses. Can you imagine blood five to six feet deep in a valley 180 miles long? When I was in Israel, a guide pointed to a valley that separates the Mount of Olives from the East Gate. It runs right up to Megiddo. Megiddo is the site where the Battle of Armageddon will be fought. How long is this valley today? It is about 200 miles long, and the Bible says the valley of blood will be 180 miles in length. Could it be the same valley? I think so. I am also thoroughly convinced that the blood will literally be up to the bridles of the horses because so often in the book of Revelation it says, "it is **like** blood." Here it says, "**it is blood**." I believe the world will know a real blood bath.

We do not have to go through this terrible time. That is wonderful to know! Christ would not send His bride through the time of Tribulation. The bride is to cleanse herself just based on loving Him; everyone who loves Him will purify himself according to 1 John 3:1-3.

According to Revelation 16, He now brings forth the seven bowls which contain the wrath of God. The first bowl contains such great pain for men that they will question if life can go on. In the second one, the sea is affected again. In the fourth bowl, men will be scorched with fire, darkness will come, etc. Finally, we come to the Battle of Armageddon.

Let me ask again, are you ready if Christ were to come? There is not one thing left to be fulfilled. The next event on God's agenda is the catching out of the church; nothing else must occur first. Israel has been reborn. Russia is brought to power. The throne of David is set. Are you ready if Christ were to come today? If you know Christ as Savior, are you really living as though He might come today?

Are We Living As If He Could Come Today?

I want to tell you a story about an American man who had a dream. This man dreamed that he died and went to heaven. When he got there, he looked at a fellow on his left and asked him, "Well, who are you and how did you get here?" And the man said, "I was a Roman. I got saved all the way back in the first century. I saw some of the early Christians martyred, and it was during that time I accepted Christ. Because I was Roman and had accepted Christ, Nero decided that I would burn; I would be a candle in one of his gardens." And the American said, "How awful!" The Roman Christian responded, "Oh, do not think it was awful. My Savior gave His life for me. Why shouldn't I give my life for Him?"

Then the American turned to the man on his right and asked, "Where did you come from and when did you get here?" The man responded, "I've only been here about 300 years. I lived on a South Sea island, and there came a time when a missionary by the name of John Williams came to our island and began to tell the gospel story about how Christ loved us and died for us. My people took that missionary and put him to death; but, before they did, I heard his message and believed him. I was so hated by my own people that I was eaten by them." And the American said, "How terrible!" The islander said, "No, not really. The missionary told me that Christ gave His life for me. Why shouldn't I die for Him?"

Almost simultaneously these two men turned and looked at the American and said, "Where did you come from, and when did you get here?" The American had a very difficult time explaining to them how "difficult" it was to live for Christ in the middle of America in the 1990s. With this, the American woke up from his dream and found that he was not in heaven at all; rather, he was in his nice, air-conditioned bedroom, between satin sheets. He had trouble sleeping the rest of the night.

I wonder, how will we give account of ourselves when we stand before God? If the Bible is true, and I believe it is, the most fearsome time of judgment is ahead for the world. That's why I say, again, do you know Christ as your Savior? While there is still time, will you receive Him?

The Church Will Not Go Through the Tribulation

In this chapter, I want to approach a very difficult and controversial subject. I am sure some of the readers of this book already have a different view than I on the subject. Everyone is entitled to his own opinion, but I want to go to the Scriptures and ask the question, "Does the church go through the Tribulation?" This is such an important question. If the church goes through the Tribulation, we certainly need to be prepared for it; but if the church is to be Raptured prior to the Tribulation, then we need to have a completely different perspective on how we should live here and now.

To be very honest, the greatest compliment anyone could give me about this book would be: "I have changed my lifestyle because I believe Christ is coming soon." I really do not want to just give out new facts. I have found that even though people may get excited about a new fact, if it never changes their thinking, if it never changes their lives, if it never changes their priorities, it is empty! I did not design this book on Bible prophecy to entertain, but to encourage people to take heed and really live as if Christ could come **today**! I pray that you are ready for Him.

In previous chapters, we have been looking at a whole collection of issues related to the soon return of Christ. We have read some prophecies in the Bible that were written 4,000 years ago, and we have begun to see those things fulfilled just in the last two or three years. We have read in 2 Peter 1:19 how God's Word is a sure word of prophecy. We have seen pointers and indicators of things to come and have seen that Christ will return for His bride. But how close **is** the coming of Christ?

How Important Is the Pre-Tribulation View?

There are several views on the subject of the Tribulation and the Rapture, Christ's return for the church. There are some that say the Rapture occurs midway through the Tribulation, and there are some that hold a post-Tribulation view. In other words, some believe the church will be Raptured after the Tribulation. There are even some that say only those who are looking for the coming of Christ will be Raptured before the Tribulation, and the rest will be Raptured at the end of the Tribulation. Then there are those, and I am among them, who believe the church will be Raptured before the Tribulation. This view is called the pre-Tribulation view. There is also a new view called pan-Tribulation. You probably have not heard of that one yet. This is the view that it does not really matter whether it is pre- or post-; it will all "pan" out in the end! A bad joke, perhaps, but it is the position that some take.

The pre-Tribulation view of the return of Christ is in agreement with what we have already learned! We have seen that the church age began on the Day of Pentecost and will end when Christ returns for the church. We know that immediately after the Rapture, the church will go the Judgment Seat of Christ, followed by the Marriage Supper of the Lamb. At the same time the church is in heaven enjoying a marriage and a honeymoon, on earth those who are not believers will go through the Tribulation. This is the basis of the pre-Tribulation view of the return of Christ.

We need to look at several passages of scripture as we consider the importance of the pre-Tribulation view. The first one is Titus 2:11: *"For the grace of God that bringeth salvation hath appeared to all men."*

In other words, no one has an excuse. People will say, "What about the person in Africa who has never heard?" Look at the verse again: *"For the grace of God that bringeth salvation hath appeared to all men."* This is a remarkable statement! It says that God, through His people, has brought the gospel to every country. They may have rejected it, but it has been brought to them. I am more worried about the people in America who reject the Word than I am about people in Africa because we have heard it more than any other people and have more responsibility for what we've heard.

"Teaching us that, denying ungodliness and worldly lusts, we should live soberly, righteously, and godly, in this present world" (vs. 12). Why should we live this way? Because this present age will soon end. *"Looking for that blessed hope, and the glorious appearing of the great God and our Saviour Jesus Christ"* (vs. 13). Notice that it says we have blessed hope, and that hope is the appearing of Jesus Christ.   Another important scripture to consider is Ephesians 4:4: *"There is one body, and one Spirit, even as ye are called in one hope of your calling."* The body is the church--one body, one church, one hope.

Now let us pause and consider the importance of these verses. According to Ephesians 4, the church has one hope. What is your hope? I have talked to people, and they have said, "Well, to be honest, my hope is that I'll die and go to heaven." That cannot be the hope that is talked about here, because I Corinthians 15:51 says that we shall not all die. *"We shall not all sleep, but we shall all be changed."*

I know of some people that say, "My hope is that I will

have everlasting life some day." This cannot be the hope referred to in Ephesians 4 as our one hope because John 3:36 says, *"He that believeth on the Son hath everlasting life: and he that believeth not the Son shall not see life; but the wrath of God abideth on him."* Salvation, everlasting life, is a present possession, not a future hope.

I Peter I says that our hope is in heaven, but it is not heaven itself. Titus 2:13 says we have one hope; it is the appearing of Jesus Christ. I John 3:2-3 says, *"Beloved, now are we the sons of God, and it doth not yet appear what we shall be: but we know that, when he shall appear, we shall be like him; for we shall see him as he is. And every man that hath this hope in him purifieth himself, even as he is pure."*

I have found that people who really believe that Christ may come pre-Tribulation live differently. You see, if we are to be Raptured midway in the Tribulation, or if we are to be Raptured after we have gone through the Tribulation, we might as well relax now. That is the thinking of a lot of people. If we really thought He could come today, we would live differently, wouldn't we?

I believe when we meet Him in the air, we will look on a face like we have never seen in all of our lives. I think we will meet a most glorious, beautiful sight that is beyond our imagination. I believe that five seconds after we have been in His presence, everything on the earth will grow so dim and distant and so dark and dreary that we will not be able to imagine how we could have had our whole existence and dreams wrapped up here. Our hope is in His appearing, and because we see His coming we pursue holy living. "Everyone who has this hope in him purifies himself." The church is to become pure just by believing that He will soon come.

Remember in the last chapter we compared the coming of Christ to a Jewish wedding. We saw that a Jewish man leaves his father's home, pays the price for his bride-to-be, seals that bargain by drinking a cup, then goes back to his father's house. In his father's house, he builds a dwelling place, he goes back for the bride, and gives a shout. The bride's only task during the time that he has been building a home is just to get herself ready for when he comes for her. The church is to be prepared, to be ready, for Christ's return.

The Church Is To Be Prepared

In the neighborhood where I grew up, there was a fellow everyone liked. For some reason, this gem of a guy fell in love with one of the girls in the neighborhood. They pledged themselves and decided that they would get married when he returned from the military service. When he got an unexpected leave, he returned unannounced and went right to her house. Her mother answered the door and said, "What in the world are you doing here?" He responded, "I had a few days off, so I thought I would surprise my bride-to-be and come home so we could get married. Is she here?" The girl's mother said the girl had gone to the store, so the young man sat down to wait. It got later and later, and at about 1:00 in the morning he was finally getting the picture. Just as he was leaving, a car pulled into the driveway. The young serviceman saw two people get out of the car. They began giggling as they made their way toward the porch, until the girl looked up and saw her fiance. She responded with shock, "What in the world are you doing here?" He said, "I thought I would surprise you and come back so we could get married."

Can you imagine the shock many Christians would feel if Christ were to come today? Just as it was difficult for that girl to explain why she was out at that time of night with another young man, so some Christians might have a hard time explaining how they've used their time during Christ's absence from earth. I believe that it is important for us to understand that Christ could come at any moment.

Every writer of a New Testament epistle gives the message of the immediate return of Christ. Notice I Thessalonians 4:16-18: *"For the Lord himself shall descend from heaven with a shout, with the voice of the archangel, and with the trump of God: and the dead in Christ shall rise first: Then we which are alive and remain shall be caught up together with them in the clouds, to meet the Lord in the air: and so shall we ever be with the Lord. Wherefore comfort one another with these words."* These are important words! From the time of the Rapture on, notice it is always this for the believer: "I am with Christ." But also notice that all the New Testament epistle writers have the same thought regarding Christ's soon return. Paul says in I Thessalonians 4:15, *"...we which are alive and remain unto the coming of the Lord shall not prevent them which are asleep."* Notice that Paul thought he would be among those that would be alive when Christ came. He says, *"...**we** which are alive...."* Paul really believed that the coming of Christ was so close that he would be alive when it came! Paul was not the only one.

Look at what John wrote in I John 2:28: *"And now, little children, abide in him; that, when he shall appear, we may have confidence, and not be ashamed before him at his coming."* John said, "I am waiting for his coming."

James says in chapter 5:8: *"Be ye also patient; stablish your hearts: for the coming of the Lord draweth nigh."* Look at Peter's words in I Peter 4:7: *"But the end of all things is at hand: be ye therefore sober, and watch unto prayer."*

Every writer of a New Testament epistle says, "The coming of Christ is close; it's here; it's now." It was to be immediate, not following the Tribulation. Christ Himself says three times in Revelation 22:7, 12, and 20, "I come quickly."

I believe if those early Christians were looking for the immediate return of Christ, we would do well to do the same.

As we look at scriptures referring to the Rapture, we never find a warning. As we looked at 1 Thessalonians 4, we saw an important emphasis. He gives the details of the coming of Christ for His bride exactly as it occurs in a Jewish wedding. The bridegroom does not send a sign back; he simply comes by the bride's window and shouts, "Let's go." She is to be ready. It is a great disgrace for a Jewish bride to be found not ready.

It would be a shame if Christ, who has a tremendous dwelling place for us, came back today and we said, "Wait a minute, one more business deal. I would like to go, but could I take the second bus up?" I do not know about you, but I cannot figure out why some people seem to want to go through part of the Tribulation. When he says, "C-O-M-E," on the "C" I'm going! I am not going to wait for a second bus. I am going on the first one! There is not one thing on my agenda that is more important than meeting Christ! Are you ready?

The Signs Are for the Tribulation

In 1 Corinthians 15:51-58, Paul says Christ will come in the twinkling of an eye. He says at the last trump He is coming without a forewarning sign, but as we recall in Matthew 24, there are lots of signs. In chapter 24:8, there is the beginning of sorrows, wars, famines, pestilence, and earthquakes in various places. We have looked at these signs in the Scriptures and have seen all of those signs coming into reality. But we should know that these signs are not for the Rapture; they are for the Tribulation. 1 Corinthians 1:22 says, *"For the Jews require a sign, and the Greeks [Gentiles] seek after wisdom."*

It is significant that Paul says the Jews require a sign

because the Tribulation is for them, and not for the Gentiles. We shall see the importance of the Tribulation and the purpose of it. In Matthew 24, while we can see the Tribulation being traced through the entire chapter, there are three "P"s to remember: the People (the Jews), the Place (Jerusalem), and the Period (Jacob's Trouble). Look at verse 15. It says, *"When ye therefore shall see the abomination of desolation, spoken of by Daniel the prophet, stand in the holy place...."* This is the Temple, and so I think we will see that indeed it is the Tribulation period of time to which Matthew refers.

Verse 29 says, *"Immediately after the tribulation of those days...."* So verse 8 is the beginning of sorrows, and verse 29 is the end of sorrows, and verse 15 is in the middle of the Tribulation. The Holy Place will be desecrated exactly as the Word of God says. However, there are no signs for the coming of Christ! Every sign is for the Tribulation **only**. Believers are to be so prepared that when the shout comes, we will be ready to leave in an instant. The scripture is so clear in this regard!

Let's look again at 1 Thessalonians and spend a little more time with that very important and precious portion of scripture, beginning with chapter 4, verses 17-18: *"Then we which are alive and remain shall be caught up together with them in the clouds, to meet the Lord in the air: and so shall we ever be with the Lord. Wherefore comfort one another with these words."*

I recently had someone, who failed to use a return address, send me a book called *The Rapture Hoax*. The book is itself a hoax, because 50 times in the gospels Christ says, "I'm coming again." He promised the disciples He would come again, and in Revelation He says no less than six times, "I am coming quickly." So if the Rapture is a hoax, then Christ is a liar. Christ is not a liar! These words are to be a promise and a comfort to the church.

In chapter 5:1 we read, *"But of the times and the seasons, brethren, ye have no need that I write unto you."* As we begin chapter 5, I want us to notice that word "but." That word is critical. Whenever we see that word, remember that what is coming after is going to be more important than what came before. If I were to say, "She is a good cook, she is an excellent singer, but..." you know what I am getting ready to do? I am getting ready to say it does not matter how she cooks or sings, because whatever I am going to say next is going to make all that was said before worthless.

As we come to this word "but" in chapter 5, it says a new topic is being introduced. Paul tells us that for those who are believers, the Rapture is the main thing. There is no need for Christians to be involved in what he is going to say next.

Now look at verses 2-3: *"For yourselves know perfectly that the day of the Lord so cometh as a thief in the night. For when they shall say...."* Notice how he's changed from "you" to "they." He was talking to "brethren," or believers. But in verse 3, he says, "When they shall say, Peace and safety." Who and what does that refer to? That is the signing of the treaty by Israel as prophesied in Daniel 9:27. Israel will be so confident of peace and safety that she will set down her arms. Israel is not disarmed today, but when the Antichrist comes, he will cause Israel to set down her arms. Then Russia will seize the opportunity and invade Israel.

"For when they shall say, Peace and safety; then sudden destruction cometh upon them, as travail upon a woman with child; and they shall not escape. But ye, brethren, are not in darkness, that that day should overtake you as a thief. Ye are all the children of light, and the children of the day: we are not of the night, nor of darkness" (vss. 3-5). He says, "The Tribulation is darkness, you are the light." The Tribulation is for the unsaved, and not for Christians.

"Therefore let us not sleep, as do others; but let us watch and be sober. For they that sleep sleep in the night; and they that be drunken are drunken in the night. But let us, who are of the day, be sober, putting on the breastplate of faith and love; and for an helmet, the hope of salvation. For God hath not appointed us to wrath, but to obtain salvation by our Lord Jesus Christ." These are powerful statements! Notice the contrast of light and darkness, sleeping and watching, drunkenness and soberness, lost and saved, the Tribulation and the Rapture, salvation and wrath. Do you see that these are opposites? Clearly, the Christians will be Raptured, and the unsaved must go into the Tribulation. He speaks of those that would be snatched out; but for those that are left behind, wrath and darkness will come. Anyone who is saved will not go through it! It is wonderful to know that if we have received Christ, we do not have to go through the Tribulation.

The Wrath of God: Not for the Church

Examine more closely the word "wrath." I want us to notice that in verse 9 it says, *"For God hath not appointed us to wrath, but to obtain salvation by our Lord Jesus Christ."* Also 1 Thessalonians 1:9-10: *"For they themselves shew of us what manner of entering in we had unto you, how you turned to God from idols to serve the living and true God; And to wait for his Son from heaven, whom he raised from the dead, even Jesus, which delivered us from the wrath to come."*

As we begin to look at these verses, we notice that He will save us from the **wrath** to come.

Next, notice the word "from." There are two different Greek words that are translated "from." One of those words is called *ektero*, which means to save us "out of"; the other words is *en*, which means to save us "through." For example, if you were walking with a child down the street and you came to a mud puddle and you grabbed his hands and lifted him up, you have saved him "from" the mud puddle. This would be the word *ektero*. Now, if you grabbed his hand and he continued to wade right through the mud puddle, you have taken him "through" the mud puddle. This would be the word *en*. Christ says, "I am going to save you; you are not appointed unto wrath. You are appointed to salvation." In this scripture, Paul says Christ has delivered us from the wrath to come, and the word he uses for "from" is the word *ektero*. "I am going to save you 'out of' the wrath to come!"

Do Christians go through the Tribulation? In Revelation it says at least four times that the Tribulation is the wrath of God. Would it be fair for God's wrath to be poured out on Christ on the cross for our sins, and then for us to be judged again by going through the wrath of God in the Tribulation? I believe the church will be gone before the Tribulation begins.

Look at a few more scriptures on wrath. *"For God hath not appointed us to wrath, but to obtain salvation by our Lord Jesus Christ"* (1 Thess. 5:9). *"But God commendeth his love toward us, in that, while we were yet sinners, Christ died for us"* (Rom. 5:8). That is incredible! When we were just as terrible as we could possibly be, Christ loved us and died for us. Look at verse 9: *"Much more then, being now justified by his blood, we shall be saved from wrath through him."* The word used for "from" is *ektero*, "out of." We are not going through wrath; He went through wrath for us. If the Tribulation is the wrath of God poured out on the earth, what would we be doing there? Our sin has already been judged. What a blessed hope we have! Comfort one another with this hope.

Let's look at one final scripture on the subject of the church escaping the wrath of God. *"Because thou hast kept the word of my patience, I also will keep thee from the hour of temptation, which shall come upon all the world, to try them that dwell upon the earth"* (Rev. 3:10). Now notice that the hour of temptation will try them that dwell on the earth; it will come upon all the world. But He says, "I will keep thee from...." Guess which word for "from" is used here? *Ektero.* "You will not go 'through' it; I will Rapture you out of it."

It is wonderful to be a Christian! A person must choose to go into the Tribulation. We can choose to go into the Tribulation by rejecting Christ. By being neutral to Christ, we say, "I choose Antichrist; I prefer to go into the Tribulation." There is no neutral ground with God. We cannot straddle the fence. By not making a choice, we have already chosen Antichrist. Have you made your choice?

The Trump Shall Sound and the Church Shall be Gone!

Every once in a while, someone will say to me, "It seems like the Bible says that the church must go through part of the Tribulation, because it mentions the trump when speaking of the Rapture in 1 Corinthians 15." Verses 51-52 say, *"Behold, I shew you a mystery; We shall not all sleep, but we shall all be changed, In a moment, in the twinkling of an eye, at the last trump: for the trumpet shall sound, and the dead shall be raised incorruptible, and we shall be changed."* Some people think the last trumpet here corresponds to the seventh trumpet in Revelation.

Remember in chapter 4 we talked about the seven seals, and when the first seal is opened, the Antichrist will come out. We also learned that when the seventh (last) seal is opened, seven trumpets will come out. They announce seven more judgments. Let me show you why this reference to trumpets in Revelation cannot be the same as the trumpet in 1 Corinthians 15 and the Rapture.

First of all, it is interesting that Corinthians was written in approximately A.D. 55, and Revelation was written about A.D. 95. How could Paul quote Revelation about the last trumpet when he was writing in A.D. 55? It would seem ridiculous to think that he would do that. Instead, let me suggest a more reasonable idea. At the end of the Jewish Feast of Trumpets, there is a long blast, called the Last Trump. There are 90 of these blasts in the Feast of Trumpets, and I think it is this last trumpet sound that is referred to in 1 Corinthians.

Overall, the Jewish feasts have a lot of significance for us. Figure 1 shows that in the feast we will find new contained in the old and the old contained in the new. The feasts are remarkable in terms of pointing to what is going to happen in the New Testament. For example, the Feast of Passover mentioned in Exodus 12 is a beautiful picture of Calvary. The Feast of Passover required a lamb to be killed and its blood put on the doorpost. When the angel of death saw the blood on the doorpost, he would pass over that house. When God sees the blood Christ shed on the cross covering those who have accepted Christ's payment for sin, He causes death to pass us by, and He gives us eternal life. The Feast of Unleavened Bread, also in Exodus 12, has to do with the Lord's Supper. The Firstfruits Feast, as described in Exodus 23, has to do with Resurrection. In Leviticus 23 is the Feast of Pentecost, which has to do with the church being formed in Acts 2. In the Jewish calendar, these first four feasts cover only a three-month period. This is a picture of Christ's three years of ministry. The fifth feast is called the Feast of Trumpets, and a four-month interval occurs between the Feast of Pentecost and the Feast of Trumpets. The Feast of Trumpets is a picture of the Rapture of the church, and after it comes the Feast of Atonement, or the Glorious Appearing. Next on the Jewish calendar is the Feast of Tabernacles, representing the Millennial Reign. These seven Old Testament feasts represent a beautiful picture of the prophetic calendar of God.

I have said all this to point us to the conclusion that the

---

1. **Passover (Exod. 12:14)**
   Calvary (1 Cor. 5:7)
2. **Unleavened Bread (Exod. 12:15-18)**
   Remembrance Table (1 Cor. 5:8)
3. **Firstfruits (Exod. 23:19)**
   Resurrection (1 Cor. 15:20)
4. **Pentecost (Lev. 23:15-21)**
   Church Formed (Acts 2:1)

INTERVAL

5. **Trumpets (Lev. 23:23-25)**
   Rapture (1 Cor. 15:52)
6. **Atonement (Lev. 16:30)**
   Glorious Appearing (Heb. 9:28)
7. **Tabernacles (Exod. 23:16)**
   Millennium (Rev. 20:1-6)

Figure 1: The Old Testament Feasts As They Picture New Testament Events

---

trumpet that will sound at the coming of Christ is from a parallel of the Feast of Trumpets. It is not the seventh trump in Revelation. The seven trumpets in Revelation announce judgment on all those in the Tribulation, but the church has been taken to heaven by Christ before any one of them begins.

Old Testament Pictures of Christ and His Return

There are other glorious pictures in the Old Testament that point us to the return of Christ and the Rapture of the church. We usually skip over chapters in the Bible like Genesis 5 which lists genealogies, but these are very important. For example, it is there in Genesis 5 that we learn Adam lived 930 years. We learn that Enoch was born 622 years after Adam was created. We read that Enoch lived 365 years, and he was taken--he was raptured! (See Figure 2 for a summary of the ages of men from Adam to Noah.)

By studying Genesis 5, we learn that when Enoch was 65 years old, he had a son by the name of Methuselah who is distinguished as being the person who lived longer than any other man. When Methuselah was 187 years old, he had a son by the name of Lamech; and when Lamech was 182 years old, he had a son by the name of Noah. When Noah was 600 years old, the flood came, but God saved Noah and his family. From the chart in Figure 2 we can see that Enoch, Methuselah, and Lamech had the opportunity to talk with Adam. Sometimes we lose that perspective as we begin to read through the book of Genesis.

As we put these men and their lives in the proper time frame, we will find that prior to the judgment of God with the flood, the Rapture of Enoch occurred. By looking at Methuselah's life, we see that in the very year of the flood, Methuselah died. It is significant also that Methuselah's name means "when it comes he shall die." What a name to give a child!

Enoch is a picture of the church and those who will be Raptured. Notice that Enoch was taken prior to the judgment of the flood. Methuselah is a picture of those who die preceding the Tribulation. Noah is a picture of a Jewish remnant that will be spared according to Zechariah 13:9. The

Bible has many such exciting pictures of the pre-Tribulation Rapture of the church. What a plan and perfect timing God has!

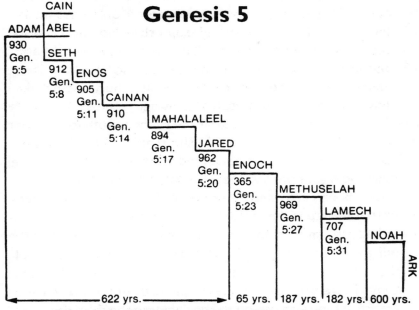

Genesis 5

CAIN
ADAM | ABEL
930 Gen. 5:5
SETH
912 Gen. 5:8
ENOS
905 Gen. 5:11
CAINAN
910 Gen. 5:14
MAHALALEEL
894 Gen. 5:17
JARED
962 Gen. 5:20
ENOCH
365 Gen. 5:23
METHUSELAH
969 Gen. 5:27
LAMECH
707 Gen. 5:31
NOAH
ARK

←———— 622 yrs. ————→ | 65 yrs. | 187 yrs. | 182 yrs. | 600 yrs.

Figure 2: The Ages of Men From Adam to Noah Based on Genesis 5.

Another wonderful picture is found in the life of Moses. In his role as a deliverer, Moses is a picture of the Lord Jesus Christ. It is interesting that while Moses was gone from the people of Israel, he was in Gentile territory. Before he came back to deliver the Jews from the persecution of Egypt, he took a Gentile bride. That is exactly what Christ is doing right now! He was rejected by Israel, so He took a Gentile bride, and He will come back and deal again with the Jewish people in the Tribulation.

Joseph's life gives us another picture of Christ. Christ was sold, even as Joseph was sold by his brothers. Like Joseph, the Lord Jesus continued to have a heart for His people. In the story of Joseph, eventually his brothers came back for food, bowed down to worship him, and he revealed himself to them. They bowed down to him as their savior. There is a day coming when the Jews will bow down to Christ as Messiah, the Savior of all. But before Joseph revealed himself to his brothers, and while he was still rejected by his own, he took his Gentile bride. The church is the Gentile bride for Christ. What a parallel the Bible gives us for the church being taken as a bride before God deals with Israel in the Tribulation!

It is interesting to look at the story of Ruth for another picture of a Gentile bride. In the story of Ruth, Boaz is a picture of Christ. The book of Judges tells us that when Israel was undergoing persecution for not possessing the Promised Land, Boaz purchased a Gentile bride named Ruth. What a remarkable parallel to Christ choosing a Gentile bride (the church) because Israel rejected Christ when He preached the kingdom to them! (See Matt. 10:5-6; 11:20-24; 21:43; 27:21-25.)

There are also wonderful pictures in the New Testament. In John 2, it says on the beginning of the third day, there was a marriage in Canaan of Galilee. Remember, for 2,000 years (two days) He set aside the Jewish people. The church age has lasted for almost 2,000 years. At the beginning of the third day he says there will be a wedding. There it is--at the end of 2,000 years, the Marriage Supper of the Lamb. What an exciting day and time for us to be living in!

The gospel of John is amazing! In every chapter there is a prophetic pointer to the fact that Christ is coming soon. One of these is in John 21, where we see the large catch of fish. Ever wonder why they caught 153 fish? Why would John give the exact number if it was not important? Some people think that it refers to the number of nations that will be in the world. In 1983 a survey was conducted that found there were

154 nations in the world. Out of the sea, which the Bible often uses as a picture of mankind in general, they caught 153 fish, but Jesus already had one fish on the fire--154 fish in all. Again, some think that the one fish on the fire may represent the nation of Israel during the Tribulation.

The entire book of John points us to Christ's coming. In John 4, Christ is walking through Samaria. Samaria was to be avoided by the Jews, but verse 4 says that He had to go there. The disciples almost assuredly reminded Him that Samaria was not friendly territory, but He said, "We must go." When they got there, He sat down at a well and began to talk to a Samaritan woman while the disciples left to get food. That day the Samaritan woman received Christ as Savior, and she ran back to the village telling the people, "I've found Christ! I've found the Messiah who can tell us all things!" The villagers came and believed His message, and it says that He went to them, and He abode with them two days, perhaps picturing the 2,000-year period of grace. After that two-day period, the Bible says He went back to the Jewish people. The New Testament is full of amazing parallels and pictures of God's plan!

Daniel Pictures Christ and His Return

Let's now look at Daniel 9 and read another very important passage of scripture. Verse 24 gives us the background: *"Seventy weeks are determined upon thy people and upon thy holy city, to finish the transgression, and to make an end of sins, and to make reconciliation for iniquity, and to bring in everlasting righteousness, and to seal up the vision and prophecy, and to anoint the most Holy."*

It actually means 70 periods of seven. In our language the only word for a period of seven is "week," so it has been translated "70 weeks." If we multiply 70 by 7, we get 490, so it is actually 490 years. I want us to notice that at the end of these 490 years, there are seven things that will be accomplished. There will be a finish of transgression and an end of sin. They will make reconciliation for iniquity, bring in everlasting righteousness, seal up the vision, fulfill prophecies, and anoint the most Holy. We are not at this point yet. I believe we have documented this in previous chapters.

Look at verses 25-27: *"Know therefore and understand, that from the going forth of the commandment to restore and to build Jerusalem unto the Messiah the Prince shall be seven weeks, and threescore and two weeks: the street shall be built again, and the wall, even in troublous times. And after threescore and two weeks shall Messiah be cut off, but not for himself: and the people of the prince that shall come shall destroy the city and the sanctuary; and the end thereof shall be with a flood, and unto the end of the war desolations are determined. And he shall confirm the covenant with many for one week: and in the midst of the week he shall cause the sacrifice and the oblation to cease, and for the overspreading of abominations he shall make it desolate, even until the consummation, and that determined shall be poured upon the desolate."*

It says we can calculate the time from the commandment to rebuild Jerusalem until Messiah the Prince, and it will be 490 years. The 490 years begins with a command to begin rebuilding Jerusalem, and ends when Christ begins to rule in the Millennium. Of that 490 years, the Bible says that 69 periods of seven will take place between the commandment to rebuild Jerusalem and when the Prince is cut off. If we were to go back to Nehemiah 2, we would find a specific time when Artaxerxes said to build the city of Jerusalem again. The clock begins, and the Bible even gives the date--the first of Nisan. If we count the number of days from that day until Christ rides through Jerusalem on the colt (recorded in Matthew

21), those days are exactly equal to 483 years--exactly 69 periods of seven. It is not off by one day! That is why it said, *"Know therefore and understand."* It says after this period of 69 periods of seven occurs, Messiah will be cut off, or He will be crucified. Did that occur? It certainly did! It says that Jerusalem will be torn down, and the city destroyed. Did that occur? It sure did when the Romans came into Jerusalem in A.D. 70. But then it says that the last period of seven will not begin until the Antichrist makes a covenant with many (the Jews) for one week. This 490 years is for the Jewish people and for Jerusalem. It is like a countdown for a launch; and as they are counting down, all of a sudden, they have to stop because there is a problem. They do not go all the way back to the beginning and start over, do they? No, they repair the rocket and begin the countdown right where they left off. In this period of 490 years, when the Jews rejected Messiah, Christ turned to the Gentiles and formed a bride composed of believers called the church, and then His plan went on.

In the gospels Christ said, "I will go to the Gentiles." Remember the story in Luke 14? He said, "I will invite them (the Jews) into the feast, and if they won't come, I will go to the highways and bring in every poor, lame, and blind person." He invited the Gentiles to come and have salvation. I thank God for it! But there's coming a day when He will Rapture the church; He will bring his bride home and then He will come back and deal with the Jews again.

Jeremiah 30:7 calls this the time of "Jacob's trouble." The church is never referred to as Jacob's. The time of Jacob's trouble is the Tribulation, and it is for the Jewish people. It will be a time when God will refine Israel, and they will turn to Christ as their Messiah, exactly as the Old Testament prophets prophesied hundreds of years ago.

More about this subject is found in Acts 15:14-16:

"Simeon hath declared how God at the first did visit the Gentiles, to take out of them a people for his name. And to this agree the words of the prophets; as it is written, After this I will return, and will build again the tabernacle of David, which is fallen down; and I will build again the ruins thereof, and I will set it up."

Several things are important here. I want us to notice that the spokesman is James. In verse 14 James says that God first called a people for His name. Who would that be? The church! We are named Christians--after His name--aren't we? He is the head of the church, and we are the body. In verse 15 James says the Old Testament is in agreement with this. If Israel rejects Messiah, Christ will turn to the Gentiles. Notice verse 16: *"After this I will return, and will build again the tabernacle of David."* Who will worship at the tabernacle of David? Gentiles? No, but the Jews will. Do you see the plan? He came to the Jews. The Jews rejected the Messiah, so He went to the Gentiles, and the church was formed. When the church is gone, claimed, and sealed, Christ will deal again with the Jewish people. That is the plan of God as stated thousands of years ago. What a wonderful plan it is! How remarkable to see the plan of God being fulfilled!

The Book of Revelation
Tells of Christ and His Return

Again, let's look at the book of Revelation and see what it has to say about the return of Christ. Whenever we read the book of Revelation, we should realize that the word revelation means "to reveal, to open up." This book was written so we could see and know the plan of God, and how it reveals the Lord Jesus Christ for all the world to see. It is not a scary book, but a blessed book. In 1:1-3 we read, *"The Revelation of Jesus Christ, which God gave unto him, to shew unto his servants things which must shortly come to pass."* There is a blessing just for reading this book. There is also a second blessing: *"And they that hear the words of this prophecy."* The word "hear" actually means "to obey." There now follows a third blessing to those that *"keep those things which are written therein: for the time is at hand."* In other words, in the very age we are in, these things will be. It's not for the next age, it's for right now. *"And he sent and signified it by his angel unto his servant John: Who bare record of the word of God, and of the testimony of Jesus Christ, and of all things that he saw. Blessed is he that readeth."*

Blessed is he that reads, blessed is he that obeys it, and blessed is he that lives in the light of it. Are you enjoying these blessings? This book and its three special blessings are for us today!

With this as a brief background, let's read Revelation 1:19, where we find a divine master outline for the book of Revelation. It is such a simple outline, but with it we can have a real grasp of what goes on throughout the entire book. He says, *"Write the things which thou hast seen, and the things which are, and the things which shall be hereafter."* In other words, the book of Revelation is going to reveal things to us from three perspectives.

1. It will show us some things that are past. This refers to chapter 1 where the clearest picture of Christ in all the Bible is given.
2. We will see things which are in the present and going on right now in the church age. I believe this description is in Revelation 2:1 to 4:1. Since Revelation was written in A.D. 95, and the church began on the Day of Pentecost (Acts 2) and continues until today, A.D. 95 would certainly be in the church age.
3. Next, he says, "Then I want to show you the things

which shall be hereafter," or future things. This section begins with chapter 4 and continues throughout the rest of the book of Revelation. Notice particularly the word "hereafter" in 1:19. That word is really the phrase *meta touta*. It is a significant word, as we shall soon see.

If you were to read the details of chapters 2 and 3, you would find that He describes seven churches. and these seven churches of Asia are historical; they really existed.

These seven churches are also typical of local churches in the church age. The description of these churches in Revelation accurately pictures seven types of people which can be found in any given local church today. There are those like the people at Ephesus who have left their first love. There are those like in Smyrna who are suffering. There are those like at the church in Philadelphia, the church of brotherly love. There are also those like in Laodicea, false professors. They talk about Christ and the Bible, but they have never received Christ as their personal Savior.

These seven churches are also prophetic. If we were to study the church at Ephesus, we would see it is most like the church in the first century. The next church mentioned, the church at Smyrna, is a picture of the time period in the church age when the church suffered. Progressing down the list, I think we would have to say that the professing church today is pictured best by the church of Laodicea with its false professors. There is a clear picture of the progression of the church down through the ages as represented by these seven churches in Revelation.

Revelation 4:1 says, *"After this I looked, and, behold, a door was opened in heaven: and the first voice which I heard as it were of a trumpet talking with me; which said, Come up hither, and I will shew thee things which must be hereafter."* Doesn't that sound like 1 Corinthians 15 and 1 Thessalonians 4? A trumpet sounds, and a voice calls out an invitation. Could I be so bold as to say that this indicates the Rapture of the church?

Notice the first two words in 4:1: "After this." Guess what these words are. They are *meta touta*. Remember from chapter 1:19 that there are three divisions, and the last one was *meta touta*, or "hereafter." As John writes Revelation 4:1, I believe he is introducing us to the last main point of the master outline. In other words, the present church age ends at the close of chapter 3, and chapter 4 begins the final division that describes those events **after** the church age has concluded. Now look at the last word in chapter 4:1. It is the word "hereafter." It is *meta touta* again. Do you see how this word tips us off that the church age is over as we begin Revelation 4?

Look again in Acts 15 at the summary of James where he said because Israel rejected the Messiah, Christ went to all the nations. In verse 16 it says, "after this" the Tabernacle of David will be built. This will occur during the Tribulation period of time. That is where the Antichrist will set up his kingdom of desecration. But it is "after this"--after what?--after the church age.

Returning to Revelation, I want to look at 2:17: *"He that hath an ear, let him hear what the Spirit saith unto the churches."* Every time He speaks to the seven churches we find a phrase like this. For another example, look at 2:11: *"He that hath an ear, let him hear what the Spirit saith unto the churches."* For each of the seven messages to those seven churches, we find this message, but look at Revelation 13:9. It says, *"If any man have an ear, let him hear."*

Notice something missing? It doesn't say to the church, does it? Why? Because the church is gone. What happened to it? It was Raptured. When? Chapter 4, verse 1 tells us that "after this" John hears the sound of a trumpet, he hears a tremendous voice, and he hears the invitation to "Come up here." John is a picture of all the believers in the church age. What a wonderful picture this is of the Rapture!

For our final argument of why the church will not go through the Tribulation, I want us to look at the scenario of chapters 4, 5, and 6 of Revelation. I believe that if we follow this closely, it will remove any doubt we may have as to whether the church goes through any part of the Tribulation. I believe emphatically that the church will not go through one second of the Tribulation! The church is to be looking for the appearing of Jesus Christ and not for a sign.

Revelation 4:1 is one of the most splendid scenes in all the Word of God! John has already described things of the past (chapter 1) and conditions in the church age (chapters 2 and 3) that exist right now. When he comes to chapter 4, he says, *meta touta*, or "after this" and "hereafter." We do not find mention of the church in the book of Revelation again until Revelation 19 when Christ comes back **with** the church at the Battle of Armageddon. Verse 1 begins with the trumpet sounding and the invitation to "Come up here!" Then the church is gone!

"And immediately [Remember the time frame of I Corinthians 15? The twinkling of an eye.] *I was in the spirit: and, behold, a throne was set in heaven, and one sat on the throne. And he that sat was to look upon like a jasper and a sardine stone"* (Rev. 4:2-3). Imagine looking at a glowing diamond and a flaming red ruby stone! In other words, the brilliance of Him that was on the throne was so great, it was likened to the sun shining on a diamond set in a ruby.

About this time, we might think that John needs to describe things a little more clearly. However, he is looking at a heavenly scene, and it is impossible to use earthly words to describe the incredible things he is seeing. It will be the most splendid sight any of us has ever seen!

He goes on in verse 3: *"And there was a rainbow round about the throne, in sight like unto an emerald."* Here we see more beauty and splendor described! *"And round about the throne were four and twenty seats: and upon the seats I saw four and twenty elders sitting, clothed in white raiment; and they had on their heads crowns of gold"* (vs. 4).

I want us to notice chapter 5:6: *"And I beheld, and, lo, in the midst of the throne and of the four beasts, and in the midst of the elders, stood a Lamb."* In the New Testament, Christ is always described as being in the midst of the church. I believe that the elders are a picture of the church. The church, we are told in Revelation 3:21, will sit on a throne. We know from Revelation 19 and 20 that the church will be clothed in white. We know that the church will be given crowns, and that Christ is always in the midst of the church. The description of these elders says they are sitting on thrones, are dressed in white, have on crowns, and Christ is in the midst. They have to represent the church, don't they?

Notice in chapter 4, verse 8 that when they are sitting on the thrones with the crowns on their heads, four living creatures come and say, *"Holy, holy, holy, Lord God Almighty, which was, and is, and is to come."* Verses 9-11 say: *"And when those beasts give glory and honour and thanks to him that sat on the throne, who liveth for ever and ever, The four and twenty elders fall down before him that sat on the throne, and worship him that liveth for ever and ever, and cast their crowns before the throne, saying, Thou art worthy, O Lord, to receive glory and honour and power: for thou hast created all things, and for thy pleasure they are and were created."*

In chapter 5, verse 1, it says: *"And I saw in the right hand of him that sat on the throne a book written within and on the* backside, sealed with seven seals." I believe this scroll is the scroll of Daniel 12 that we looked at earlier where God said, "Daniel, seal up the book because it is so terrible." In that scroll were the judgments of the Tribulation. Daniel fainted because it was so terrible that he couldn't even bear to read it. Could it be possible that judgments of this nature and magnitude could happen on the earth? By the way, the last will and testimony of a Roman during Bible times was normally on a scroll sealed with seven seals. This seven-sealed scroll discussed in Revelation will be like the last will of God for the earth.

Now consider Revelation 5:2: *"And I saw a strong angel proclaiming with a loud voice, Who is worthy to open the book, and to loose the seals thereof?"* The scroll contains the Title Deed to all the earth. *"And no man in heaven, nor in earth, neither under the earth, was able to open the book, neither to look thereon"* (vs. 3). In verse 4 John begins to weep, but one of the elders says in verse 5, *"Weep not: behold, the Lion of the tribe of Judah, the Root of David, hath prevailed to open the book, and to loose the seven seals thereof."* Who would that be? Christ is the Lion of the tribe of Judah, and He is the Root of David.

"And I beheld, and, lo, in the midst of the throne and of the four beasts, and in the midst of the elders, stood a Lamb as it had been slain" (vs. 6). Can you think of a Lamb that has been slain and then resurrected? It has to be Christ! Look at verses 6-7. He had, *"Seven horns and seven eyes, which are the seven Spirits of God sent forth into all the earth. And he came and took the book out of the right hand of him that sat upon the throne."* There is only one person that is worthy to open up the Title Deed to all the earth. It is Christ! He will come and execute His own will and testimony!

"And when he had taken the book, the four beasts and four and twenty elders fell down before the Lamb" (vs. 8). They will

release bowls of incense, which are prayers of the saints, and they will sing a new song. In verses 11 and 12, John heard the voices of many angels around the throne, the living creatures, and the elders which numbered 10,000 times 10,000 singing praises to Christ. Thousands and thousands will be saying with a loud voice, *"Worthy is the Lamb that was slain to receive power, and riches, and wisdom, and strength, and honor, and glory,and blessing"* (vs. 12). Every creature will worship Him.

Then in chapter 6, verse 1 we read, *"And I saw when the Lamb opened one of the seals, and I heard, as it were the noise of thunder, one of the four beasts saying, Come and see."* Remember that the first thing that will happen when Christ opens the first seal is the Antichrist will come forth. But the Antichrist cannot come until the first seal is opened. Christ will not open the first seal until He takes the scroll from God (5:7). He will not take the scroll until crowns are thrown before the throne (4:10). The church cannot throw crowns before the throne until they are given out, and we cannot receive them until we are Raptured!

I think we have begun to see the trap that those who believe in a mid-Tribulation or post-Tribulation view would find themselves in if they looked carefully at Revelation 4 through 6.

Look now at 2 Timothy 4:7-8. Paul writes: *"I have fought a good fight, I have finished my course, I have kept the faith: Henceforth there is laid up for me a crown of righteousness, which the Lord, the righteous judge, shall give me at that day: and not to me only, but unto all them also that love his appearing."*

Revelation 22:12 says that when Christ comes He will bring His reward with Him. In other words, at the Rapture Christ will bring the crowns with Him for those in the church age. Paul says, "I am going to get a crown of righteousness, but it's not me only. On that day, all who love His appearing will get their crowns at that same time, at the Judgment Seat of Christ." The sequence is that the church is Raptured, the Judgment Seat of Christ occurs, and crowns are given. Then we see Him for all that He is, and we take our crowns and throw them at His feet. Christ then comes and takes the scroll and opens the first seal, and the Antichrist comes forth.

When the Antichrist comes, he will make a treaty with Israel. Until that treaty is made, the Tribulation cannot begin, and the treaty cannot be made until the Antichrist is released. But the Antichrist cannot come until the seal is broken. The seal will not be broken until first Christ gets the scroll. The scroll will not be given out until the crowns of the Christians are laid at the throne. The crowns must be worn before they are thrown, and we cannot wear our crowns until He comes in the Rapture and gives them to us.

Do you understand what this means? It cannot be pan-Tribulation; it cannot be post-Tribulation; it cannot be mid-Tribulation. Christ could come at this very second! Are you ready? The book of Revelation gives one message: the church is to be looking for Christ to come at any moment. Whether it was the church one day after Pentecost, or the church 100 years after Pentecost, or the church 1,900 years after Pentecost; the church is to be looking for Christ to come. Are you looking? Every sign that we have mentioned only says the Tribulation is coming, but He said to those that receive Him, *"I will save you from the wrath to come."* We should be looking for the soon return of Christ!

God's Plan from Christ's Birth to Eternity

Figure 3 shows the time line from Christ's birth to eternity. It should help us understand God's plan for the future. From this chart we can see that the church age began on the Day of Pentecost and will conclude with the Rapture.

After the Rapture, when Christ comes for His bride, the church goes to the Judgment Seat of Christ, followed by the Marriage Supper of the Lamb, while the people on earth go through the Tribulation. At the end of the Tribulation, Christ will come back with His bride, and then the Battle of Armageddon and the Judgment of the Nations will occur. This chart also shows the kingdom age, sometimes called the Millennium or Millennial Reign, followed by Satan's last battle and the Great White Throne Judgment.

On this chart we can see the position, in terms of time, of the four major wars which the Bible says are yet to occur. The chart also summarizes the five major judgments as recorded in the Bible. Notice that we could take the chapters of Revelation, place them in order along the time line, and they would coincide exactly with the events shown. We should be able to use this chart to help us understand God's plan for all of us in the days ahead.

Are You Sure?

Maybe you do not know if you have ever received Christ. The Bible says you can be sure. I John 5:10-11 says, *"He that believeth on the Son of God hath the witness in himself: he that believeth not God hath made him a liar; because he believeth not the record that God gave of his Son. And this is the record, that God hath given to us eternal life, and this life is in his Son."*

Eternal life is a gift, and the only way to receive that gift is to accept Christ. In Christ is life. Salvation is not doing all the good works you can do. Salvation is receiving a gift, a gift of Christ. Have you ever received Him? When you receive Christ you receive eternal life because God has placed eternal life in Christ!

I John 5:12-13 says, *"He that hath the Son hath life; and he*

From Jesus Christ's

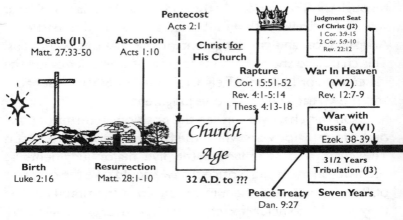

Rev. 1   Rev. 2-3   Rev. 4-5

Wars to Come

1 War with Russia (Rosh) and other nations against Israel (Ezek. 38-39/1st half of the Tribulation)

2 War in Heaven (Rev. 12:7-9/Middle of the Tribulation)

3 Battle of Armageddon (Rev. 19:17-19;16:14/End of the Tribulation

4 Final Battle with Satan; Gog and Magog (Rev. 20:7/End of the Millennium

Birth to Eternity

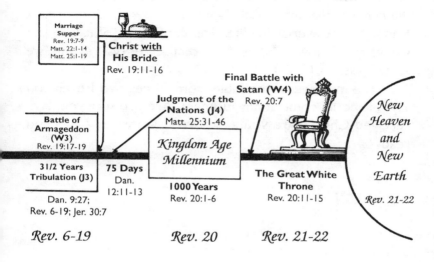

Judgments

1   Judgment for sin--Calvary ; A.D. 32

2   Judgment of believers' works--Judgment Seat of Christ (1 Cor. 3:11-15)

3   Judgment of the Jews on earth during the Tribulation (Jer. 30:7; Rev. 6-19)

4   Judgment of the nations on earth after the Tribulation (Matt. 35:31-46)

5   Judgment of the wicked dead--Great White Throne (Rev. 20:11) *that hath not the Son of God hath not life. These things have I written unto you that believe on the name of the Son of God; that ye may know that ye have eternal life, and that ye may believe on the name of the Son of God."* I am a "know-so Christian." **I know** I have everlasting life. The confidence of it is in the verses that follow: *"And this is the confidence"* (vs. 14) and *"we know"* (vss. 15,18-20).

The message of the Bible from Genesis to Revelation says He could come at any moment. Are you sure you have received Christ? Are you a "know-so Christian"? Are you ready?

The Judgment Seat of Christ

The Bible prophecy addressed in this chapter is especially for believers in our Lord Jesus Christ. Although we often use the second coming of Christ as a way to speak to the unsaved, I really believe the primary message of the return of Christ is for those who are already believers. Christ will return for the believers, and we will be snatched off the earth, but what will it be like the moment after we've been Raptured and go to the Judgment Seat?

There is a story about a poor woman who boarded a city bus with 13 wiggly, giggling, rowdy children. As she got them on the bus, the bus driver smiled and said, "Are they all yours, or is this a picnic?" The lady responded, "They are all mine, and this is no picnic!" As we consider the Judgment Seat of Christ, I am amazed that people look at it like it's going to be a Sunday School picnic. Yet, as I examine this important subject as described in the Word of God, I really believe that it's going to be a time when we will take a close inventory of how we have spent every single moment of time since we came to know Jesus Christ.

The Rapture and our reunion with Christ should be the happiest day of our lives. It should be the grandest moment of all, but will we be asking ourselves, "Why didn't I do more when the opportunity was there? Why did I spend so much time on foolish things and on things that were just for time and not for eternity?" Will we be wishing we could go back and live one month, one year, one lifetime over again? I pray those won't be our thoughts when we hear the sound of the trumpet and the voice of Christ giving the invitation, "Come up here." I really believe that day is not far off!

"We have also a more sure word of prophecy." As we have considered the incredible fulfillment of prophecy that has occurred in just the last few years, we surely have become convinced that God's Word is a sure word. We surely have come to realize that Christ could come at any moment!

A split second after the church is Raptured, every believer will stand in Christ's presence. In this chapter, we want to look at what will take place the instant after the return of Christ.

The Rapture

Before we stand in Christ's presence at the Judgment Seat of Christ, we will first be taken out of this world. In the earlier chapters of this book, we have called this the Rapture of the church. The Rapture or the "snatching up" of those who are believers is such an important event! I want us to consider the impact of the phrase "to snatch up" or "to snatch away." This phrase, or forms of it, are used in several places in God's Word. In Matthew 13:18-19, we read: *"Hear ye therefore the parable of the sower. When any one heareth the word of the kingdom, and understandeth it not, then cometh the wicked one, and catcheth away that which was sown in his heart. This is he which received seed by the wayside."*

Notice the word "catcheth." It really means "to snatch" or "to take away, to drag away." There are a number of different words that can be translated "to take away," but this particular one is "to snatch," which means to carry off suddenly with great force.

We find this word again in John 10:12: *"But he that is an*

hireling, and not the shepherd, whose own the sheep are not, seeth the wolf coming, and leaveth the sheep, and fleeth: and the wolf catcheth them, and scattereth the sheep." Again the word "catchetch" means to snatch away with great power.

In Acts 8 we find another time when this word is used. Verse 39 says, *"And when they were come up out of the water, the Spirit of the Lord caught away Philip, that the eunuch saw him no more: and he went on his way rejoicing."* An amazing scene! It occurred when Philip was having a tremendous revival in Samaria, and the Spirit of God said, "I want you to leave this revival where hundreds of people are responding to Christ, and I want you to go out into the wilderness and talk to one man." And it was in the wilderness that one man turned to Christ and was baptized because of Philip's witness. After they came up out of the water, Philip was caught away.

Now the word "caught" or "catch," whether it is in Matthew 13, or John 10, or Acts 8, is really a powerful word! There are people who contend there is no such thing as the Rapture because the word "rapture" is not in the Bible. We have just read three instances where words are translated "snatched" or "to carry off with great power." That sounds like rapture to me!

Now notice 1 Thessalonians 4:17: *"Then we which are alive and remain shall be caught up together with them in the clouds, to meet the Lord in the air: and so shall we ever be with the Lord."* Again notice the words "caught up." He will come to the clouds and snatch us away. We have read in 1 Corinthians 15:52 that this will occur in the twinkling of an eye. That's sudden, isn't it? In the Bible there are remarkable examples of the snatching away or Rapture of people. Contrary to the belief of those who say the Rapture is not in the Bible, I find at least seven instances where people were Raptured.

One of the most interesting Rapture events is in Genesis

5 involving a man named Enoch. The Bible says that after he had a son, he walked with God for 300 years. Isn't that a tremendous testimony? He walked with God for 300 years! Then it says the Lord took him. Isn't that beautiful? God was so delighted with Enoch's life that He said, "Enoch, you walk closer to Me than you walk to the people. You might as well be up here." God took him! The book of Jude says they looked for him, but they didn't find him. That was certainly a Rapture!

Another remarkable story is the life of Elijah. Elijah, a prophet of God, was taken by God. The other prophets looked for him, thinking he was hiding, but he had been taken by God.

In the New Testament we find a beautiful picture of the Lord Jesus Christ being Raptured in Acts 1:9. He was talking to the disciples, and He was taken up into heaven. In 2 Corinthians 12, Paul describes an experience of a man being caught up into the third heaven. I think it was Paul himself who was Raptured in this instance. In Revelation 4:1, John says he heard a voice, an invitation, the sound of a trumpet, and he was taken to another place. I think he was Raptured! In Revelation 11, two witnesses will be Raptured in a way that all the people on the earth will be watching! Don't be surprised if the next "example" of Rapture we see is the snatching out of the church! With great power, Christ will snatch away everyone who believes. He will catch us away. We will be raptured!

The Judgment Seat of Christ

Now, immediately after this glorious Rapture, the church will be taken to the Judgment Seat of Christ. As we look at the Judgment Seat of Christ, I believe that we need to understand right from the beginning that this is not a judgment for sin. Over 1,900 years ago, Christ was judged for our sin on the cross. We will never be judged for our sin again! Isn't that wonderful? We can be on our way to heaven because 1,900 years ago, the perfect Lamb of God bore our sin. The sin question is settled. If, however, you decide to remain neutral to Christ, God must judge you for your sin. Even though the debt was paid 1,900 years ago on the cross, you have to accept Christ to receive the benefit of Christ's sacrifice for you. The believer does not go to a judgment for sin; he goes to a judgment for his works.

Let's look at 1 Corinthians 3:10-11: *"According to the grace of God which is given unto me, as a wise masterbuilder, I have laid the foundation, and another buildeth thereon. But let every man take heed how he buildeth thereupon. For other foundation can no man lay than that is laid, which is Jesus Christ."*

Notice that the foundation is Christ. Any other foundation won't last. Verses 12-13 read, *"Now if any man build upon this foundation gold, silver, precious stones, wood, hay, stubble; Every man's work shall be made manifest: for the day shall declare it, because it shall be revealed by fire; and the fire shall try every man's work of what sort it is* [or of what motive or kind it is]."

I want us to pay particular attention to the fact that it says, "every man's work shall be made manifest." What does this mean? We know from Ephesians 2:8-9 that we are not saved by works: *"For by grace are ye saved through faith; and that not of yourselves: it is the gift of God: Not of works, lest any man should boast."*

So the Judgment Seat of Christ is not concerning salvation, is it? Let's learn more about this judgment. I Corinthians 3:14 says, *"If any man's work abide which he hath built thereupon, he shall receive a reward."* It is certainly different from salvation! Salvation is not a reward; it is a gift.

What we find described in 1 Corinthians 3 is the

Judgment Seat of Christ. It's a reward; it's a judgment based on works. It is not salvation. *"If any man's work shall be burned, he shall suffer loss: but he himself shall be saved; yet so as by fire"* (vs. 15). We can know that if we believe in Christ and are taken to be with Christ at the Rapture, the worse thing that can happen is that we will enter into heaven but won't have a single reward. We can never lose the finished work of Christ! Do you know why? Because the finished work of Christ is dependent upon the life of our Lord Jesus Christ, and His life is perfect. Isn't that wonderful to know? My salvation is secure because of the finished work of Christ, not because of me. But how we live after being saved does determine whether or not we receive rewards. Christ is coming soon, and we need to be living for Him!

We need to stop and take an inventory of how we spend our time. What are we doing? What are our goals? On our mental "tablet" we need to put one column heading with a "T" for time, and one with an "E" for eternity. We need to be reminded that once the Rapture has taken place, those things in the "T" column will be gone and of no use. We can enjoy things like baseball or basketball, and can marvel at current happenings like space flights, and there is nothing wrong with these things. But we need to remember they are only for time, and not for eternity. We will bear the marks of the Judgment Seat of Christ for the rest of eternity. The reward we receive will be for eternity and will be based on what we have done with our lives since we have received Christ.

The stage is set, and we are in the dressing room of eternity. All the preparations we make here will determine what will be for eternity. Is there anything of this past week that we were involved in that will count for eternity? The day that Christ comes back should be the happiest day of our lives. It should be the instant we've been waiting for, and it can be if we have been living for Him. But when that moment comes, it will be too late to go back and to serve Him and do those things we wish we had taken time to do. Time is only to work for Christ. How are we using our time? Are we ready for Christ's return when He will bring down the curtain on our old lives and take us into a glorious new scene in heaven? Are we preparing now for that grand entrance into eternity?

Let's look at I Corinthians 4:5: *"Therefore judge nothing before the time, until the Lord come, who both will bring to light the hidden things of darkness, and will make manifest the counsels of the hearts: and then shall every man have praise of God."* I believe that God will find something in every believer for which to praise Him. In some of us, He is going to have to look pretty hard, but He will find it. Isn't that encouraging?

In I Corinthians 9:24-25 we find further information about the coming judgment for believers: *"Know ye not that they which run in a race run all, but one receiveth the prize? So run, that ye may obtain. And every man that striveth for the mastery is temperate in all things. Now they do it to obtain a corruptible crown; but we an incorruptible."* You see the stakes? There is something that you and I are striving for right now that we can never do in eternity, and that is to live our lives for Christ. Verses 26-27 read, *"I therefore so run, not as uncertainly; so fight I, not as one that beateth the air: But I keep under my body, and bring it into subjection* [I bring my body under control]: *lest that by any means, when I have preached to others, I myself should be a castaway* [should be disapproved]."

Do you see what Paul is saying? He says that the flesh is so weak that literally he beats himself black and blue to keep his body under control. He works to control the body so he can be at his best for God's service. He is living for eternity, not for time!

In the two books of Corinthians, we find four tremendous passages on the Judgment Seat of Christ. Let's look at 2 Corinthians 5:9-10: *"Wherefore we labour, that, whether present or absent, we may be accepted of him. For we must all appear* [he is talking to believers] *before the judgment seat of Christ; that every one may receive the things done in his body, according to that he hath done, whether it be good or bad."* What a picture Paul paints! The words "judgment seat" really represent the idea of the judgment stand. In a coming day, Christ Himself will sit on a judgment stand and from there He will look at the life of every believer. He wants to see if what we have done with our body during our lifetime has been according to the Word of God. In 1 Corinthians 3, 4, and 9, He tells us, "I am going to judge your life to see what the motive was and what kind of work you did." He won't just look at the fact that you taught Sunday School, but how did you teach it? What was your motive? What was in your heart?

I believe each Christian will stand before the Judgment Seat of Christ, and each life will be reviewed. In 1 Corinthians 3:13 we see how public this review will be: *"Every man's work shall be made manifest: for the day shall declare it, because it shall be revealed by fire; and the fire shall try every man's work of what sort it is."* He will expose our works for all to see. I believe in a coming day we will see not only what we have done, but I think we will see why we did it and what the hidden motives were. This ought to bring us to our knees! I believe if we really realized how soon the coming of Christ is, how near we are to the Judgment Seat of Christ, there would be things in our lives we would change today! We dare not wait until tomorrow, Christ could come today!

I believe 1 John 1:9 is one of the most blessed promises in the Bible: *"If we confess our sins, he is faithful and just to forgive us our sins, and to cleanse us from all unrighteousness."* Isn't that wonderful? That means every vain thought, every foul deed, every incorrect motive can be confessed and forgiven! What a joy! What a God!

Now, when will the Judgment Seat of Christ take place? I believe it will occur immediately after the Rapture. In 2 Timothy 4:7 the apostle Paul says that he is going to receive a crown of righteousness. He says he'll receive it at that day and so will all those who love His appearing. Notice the time frame? On that day. Paul was expecting Christ to come in his lifetime, and the day he speaks of is the day Christ will come for the church. In Revelation 22:12 Christ says, "My reward is with me when I come." He is so anxious to reward those who have served Him that He will bring those rewards with Him when He comes! 1 Corinthians 4:5 says not to judge anything until the Lord comes, implying that when He comes He will sit in judgment.

Why does the judgment come so quickly? Because immediately after this judgment, we will go to the Marriage Supper of the Lamb. He wants the judgment taken care of beforehand. In Revelation 4, we have seen that in heaven the church will be those who are dressed in white, seated on thrones, with Christ in the midst. And we will be wearing crowns. Where do the crowns come from? John said Christ will bring them when He comes. Also remember from our study that until the crowns are given, the scroll can't be opened. If the scroll can't be opened, the Antichrist cannot be released because he is released in the first seal. We can be sure that the crowns will be given out in the air, when we go to meet Christ at His coming for His bride.

How will the rewards be determined? Revelation 22:12 says, *"To give every man according as his works shall be."* 1 Corinthians 3:8 says, *"Every man shall receive his own reward according to his own labor."* 1 Corinthians 3:13 says, *"The fire shall try every man's works."* There is a set criteria for our works. I think He will look at our lives to see what we accomplished for God. In order for anything to be useful to God or for anything we do to last, it must be built upon the foundation of Jesus Christ! Did we do it for the glory of Jesus Christ? Was He the reason behind our actions? That is the only motive that will last! I think on that day we will be surprised. We will see that many things we have done have been for our own selves. Even if our works were for good, our motives may have been selfish. Only those things built on Jesus Christ will be counted worthy of reward.

In 1 Corinthians 3 Paul says some of our works are destructible. Some of them are like wood, hay, and stubble. If we were to put a match to them, there would be nothing left but a pile of ashes when the flame died away. Some of our works are indestructible. They are like gold, silver, and precious stones. Fire doesn't hurt them. All fire does to gold is refine it. If our works are done on the foundation of Christ with a proper motive, when the fire comes, they won't be destroyed. They will endure. Will we receive a reward? Will the joy of wearing crowns be ours?

Some works appear big in the eyes of men, but don't be deceived. I believe we'll be surprised when rewards are given out. Some of the most public people, some of the preachers of prominence, may not receive a great reward. I believe that maybe some of the prayer warriors that have been unknown and back in the corner will be those who receive the greater rewards. That which may appear small to man could be so valuable and precious to the Lord Jesus. In Matthew 19:30 Christ says, *"But many that are first shall be last; and the last shall be first."* We may not be known by men on this earth, but if we live faithfully for Christ now, He will recognize us and reward us for our faithfulness.

The Victor's Crown

In the Bible there are five tremendous crowns mentioned that we can receive. We only know of these five, but there may be others as well. One is called an Incorruptible Crown, or the Victor's Crown. It's the one that we read of in 1 Corinthians 9:25: *"And every man that striveth for the mastery is temperate in all things. Now they do it to obtain a corruptible crown; but we an incorruptible."* According to this scripture, the Victor's Crown is given to those who have control over fleshly desires and lusts.

Paul says in verse 26: *"I therefore so run, not as uncertainly."* Have you ever seen someone run a race and not know where the finish line is? Can someone really run a good race if he doesn't know where the finish line is? A runner needs to know how long the race is, so he can pace himself. He needs to discipline himself for the whole race, not just for the first lap. It's not so much how we start a race, it's how we finish!

I see people come to know Christ, and for the first week they read the Bible and pray every day. Six months later, where's the prayer time? Where's the Bible reading? Paul said, "I don't run as uncertainly." He said, "I need to know where the finish line is." He had one thought in mind that I think helped him run a steady race: **Run the race like Christ is coming today!** Are we doing that? My guess is that we have spent more time today scheming about what we are going to do tomorrow, than we did living for eternity. Eternity is a lot more important than tomorrow!

Paul also says, *"So fight I, not as one that beateth the air."* If you have ever seen a boxing match where the fighter was beating the air, he was probably receiving the beating of his life from his opponent! Some of us are out there swinging, but we're not hitting anything. We carry our Bibles, but the only time we give out a gospel tract is when we are with other

Christians. We're brave talking about the Lord inside the church building. It's not the building that matters so much; it's when we go out that really counts!

Paul also tells us that he needs to bring his body under subjection in order to receive the Victor's Crown. The thing that will disqualify us from this crown is if our body gains control over eternity. How are we doing on this crown? It's tough living in America and keeping the body under control. We've got fast food restaurants at every corner. We've got so many things that are enjoyable to do. But our discipline must be a day by day, moment by moment priority. We never hear of an athlete that trains only a week at a time. They train every day, every hour, every minute. They have to bring the body under control if they want to win. If we do that in Christ, there's a crown for us. He doesn't say it's easy, but it's worth it!

The Crown of Life

There is a second crown, the Crown of Life. We read of it in James 1:12: *"Blessed is the man that endureth temptation: for when he is tried, he shall receive the crown of life, which the Lord hath promised to them that love him."* Every once in a while God allows testing, not a temptation to sin, but a testing, to come into our lives. Do you know why He does that? The testing is an opportunity for us to wear a crown for eternity. Isn't that remarkable! We look at tests in our lives all the time and say, "Oh, don't I have it bad? Oh, woe is me!" God gives us this testing as an opportunity. He says, "Listen, if you will go through the testing, and if you will do it to the glory of God, you shall receive the Crown of Life!" It's high time some of us got on our knees and said, "Thank you God for giving me an opportunity for a crown."

This crown is also for those who will endure severe

testing, even unto death. Revelation 2:10 says, *"Fear none of those things which thou shalt suffer: behold, the devil shall cast some of you in prison, that ye may be tried; and ye shall have tribulation ten days: be thou faithful unto death, and I will give thee a crown of life."* There have been believers thrown into prison because of their faith. Peter and John were among them. They preached the gospel and the resurrection of Christ, and were thrown into prison for it. Now we discover the reason: that they might be tried by being cast into prison so they could wear a Crown of Life.

Revelation 2:10 also says, *"Be thou faithful unto death."* Christians have not only known what it was to be thrown into prison, but some of them have died. They will receive the Crown of Life! So often we say, "Isn't it a shame those missionaries lost their lives right in their prime?" We should be saying, "Isn't it wonderful that God took them home, and He gave them a Crown of Life!" I envy those who can give their lives for Him and receive a Crown of Life.

The Soul Winner's Crown: The Crown of Rejoicing

Now before we begin thinking these crowns are so hard to obtain that we don't want them, let's look at Philippians 4:1: *"Therefore, my brethren dearly beloved and longed for, my joy and crown."* I think Paul was closely involved with seeing these people in Philippi come to know the Lord as Savior. He was so in love with them that he called them "dearly beloved," and he longed for them because they were his "joy and his crown." This crown might be called the Soul Winner's Crown or the Crown of Rejoicing. In I Thessalonians 2:19 we also read of this crown for those that win souls. Will that crown be yours? Remember, God is in the business of saving people. Our job is simply to give the message. I often think that when one person comes to know the Lord as Savior, there may have been a dozen people involved in one way or another. I believe each will receive a Crown of Rejoicing. There may have been someone who had been praying. There may have been someone that handed out literature. There may have been someone that said a word about the Lord Jesus. There may have been someone who had something to say that reflected well on Christ. I believe the Lord will be gracious in His rewards. Will the Crown of Rejoicing, the Soul Winner's Crown, be yours?

The Crown of Glory

We look now at 1 Peter 5:4 to learn of another crown: *"And when the chief Shepherd shall appear, ye shall receive a crown of glory that fadeth not away."* He's talking about those that are elders, to those that are involved in the spiritual leadership of the local church. For the elders who serve with proper motives, there will be a Crown of Glory. What a joy to serve the Lord!

The Crown of Righteousness

The fifth crown is described in 2 Timothy 4:6-8. This one is called the Crown of Righteousness. Paul says, *"For I am now ready to be offered, and the time of my departure is at hand. I have fought a good fight, I have finished my course, I have kept the faith: Henceforth there is laid up for me a crown of righteousness, which the Lord, the righteous judge, shall give me at that day: and not to me only, but unto all them also that love his appearing."* Isn't that remarkable? I long for this crown to be mine. I long for this crown to be obtained by every believer who reads this book.

I really believe, however, that of all five crowns, this crown will be given to the fewest number of people. The reason I say this is because I believe the Bible says when Christ omes back not even those who are saved will be looking for Him. If we were looking for Him to come and really loved His appearing, we wouldn't have to be told that we need to be winning souls. I really believe that if we loved His appearing, we wouldn't have to be told that we need to keep our fleshly desires under control. I really believe that if we thought Christ was coming today, we would live differently! To love His appearing doesn't mean to love Him. I don't doubt that every believer loves Him, but to love His appearing is to live each day in the anticipation that this may be the moment of His return.

When I see Christians that aren't excited about the coming of Christ, you know what I wonder? I wonder if they are really believers! Have they ever really accepted Christ? Let's look at it this way. If this was to be the day of your wedding, wouldn't you be excited? Wouldn't you be anxious? If we are Christians, we are to be as a bride prepared for the coming of our groom. We are the bride of Christ awaiting His soon return. I don't mind telling you, I'm anxious right now. Every time I hear a band play, I think, "Is this it? Is that the trumpet?" It's all right to be excited and anxious because I believe we are that close to when Christ will come. Do you love His appearing?

I want you to know that every dream and every ambition I have will be fulfilled when I see Him! I will see the radiant One of all the universe! I will see the one that with Words created everything we see! I will be with Him! I will be His bride! I will rule with Him! I will reign with Him! And people are excited about owning a piece of the rock on the earth! People get excited about owning an acre of ground, a house, a building, a business! It's nothing! We will rule and reign with Him over all creation! I will be a joint heir with Christ over the universe! Oh, the joy that will be mine! Christ is so excited about His bride that He anticipates the moment when we will be Raptured. For 1,900 years, He has been waiting for His bride. We should also be excited, for I believe we are on the verge of when Christ will come. We need to be living as though He will come today. We need to be preparing to receive our crowns. However, we also need to know it is possible to lose our rewards.

The Loss of Rewards

I Corinthians 3:15 says we can lose our reward, even though we are saved. This should drive every one of us to our knees in our prayer closet. "Oh, God, you know my motives. You know the hidden sins. I confess them now. Forgive me."

I John 2:28 says we can have confidence and not be ashamed before Him because of our sinful living. Maybe some of us are engaged in sinful living that would bring disgrace to the name of God. In view of the fact that Christ may come at any moment, we need to turn our lives around and seek God's forgiveness. 2 Timothy 2:5 says that we are to strive lawfully, to run the race according to the Word of God. Revelation 3:11 tells us to hold fast, be faithful. But there can be a loss of reward if we are not living a life faithful to God's Word.

The Use of the Crowns

Once we have received our crowns, what happens? The crowns are not just so that we can go to heaven and say, "Hey! I've got three crowns, and you've only got two! Aren't they pretty on me?" No, I think they are for a far greater purpose. Revelation 4:4-5 describes our first moment in heaven: *"And round about the throne were four and twenty seats: and upon the seats I saw four and twenty elders sitting, clothed in white raiment; and they had on their heads crowns of gold. And out of the throne proceeded lightnings and thunderings and voices: and there were seven lamps of fire burning before the throne, which are the seven Spirits of God."*

In verses 8-9 we read, *"And the four beasts had each of them six wings about him; and they were full of eyes within: and they rest not day and night, saying, Holy, holy, holy, Lord God Almighty, which was, and is, and is to come. And when those beasts give glory and honour and thanks to him that sat on the throne, who liveth for ever and ever."*

With our first step into heaven, we are going to see awesome things that are beyond our imagination. We are going to see the God of the Universe seated on a throne, and we will be seated on thrones around Him. We are going to be clothed in white raiment with crowns on our heads. Christ will be in our midst! Then we are going to see four beasts (living creatures) so glorious they'll be like nothing we've ever seen. Those magnificent creatures are going to begin saying, "Holy, holy, holy, Lord God Almighty." As they begin to give testimony concerning Christ, they will give worship and glory to Him. We are going to be so awed by these four living creatures and their worship unto Him, do you know what we are going to do? We are going to say, "We should worship Him too. God is worthy of our praise!"

In verses 10-11 we read, *"The four and twenty elders fall down before him that sat on the throne, and worship him that liveth for ever and ever, and cast their crowns before the throne, saying, Thou art worthy, O Lord, to receive glory and honour and power: for thou hast created all things, and for thy pleasure they are and were created."* Our beautiful crowns will be used to worship Him by casting them at His feet. In that coming day, as we see Christ, we are going to fall in love with Him. We are going to take those crowns, and we are going to say, "Listen, I want to give You the very best thing I've got. I want to give You this crown that You gave me." We will throw them at His feet in worship and praise!

Queen Elizabeth II had a crown of 2,783 diamonds, 277 pearls, 18 sapphires, 11 emeralds, and 5 rubies. All of the jewels were priceless gems; one could not buy any of them! I want you to know that any saint that has a crown on that day will have a crown more glorious than Queen Elizabeth II! That's how beautiful the crowns will be! It will be a time of praise and rejoicing as we worship God.

But all may not be joy. Can you imagine what it would be like to be in heaven and have people take their crowns and throw them at His feet and have to say, "I have none to give?" What if all we can say is, "I lived life for self. I lived it for time. I just thought about how big *my* burden was. I just thought about me! I didn't think He was coming yet. I thought I still had time. I have no crown to lay at His feet!"

Someone has spread the rumor that there will be no tears in heaven. That's not true! He said, "I will wipe away tears." That implies there will be tears. I believe that at the Judgment Seat of Christ there won't be a dry eye. For as He begins to play back the videotape of our lives--of our works, of our motives, of our hidden desires--I believe there will be tears.

A Heavenly Scene

In my own mind I try to picture what it will be like when Christ calls us out, and we go to join those believers who have died. We will meet them in the air. Then we will be with Him and receive our new bodies. I believe one by one Christ will call every saint by name, and every man individually will receive his rewards for the things he has done on earth.

Christ will call Matthew, who wrote the gospel of Matthew, and He will say, "Matthew, what have you done for

Me?" Matthew will answer, "I admit that when I was a disciple, I wasn't much of one. I know that I ran when I was in the garden. I know that when others stood by the cross, I was as far away as I could be. But you know there came a time after the resurrection that I was convinced you really were who you said you were." According to history, Matthew was asked, "Will you deny that Christ, the one you followed, rose from the dead?" Matthew said, "I cannot say what I know is not true. I cannot deny the resurrection." And they took a sword and slew Matthew in Ethiopia. Christ will say to Matthew, "Well done, thou good and faithful servant!"

James the Great was beheaded in Jerusalem. James the Less was thrown from a pinnacle of the temple and then, because he was still alive, they went down and beat him with a club until they split his body in two. Bartholomew was cut up alive. Andrew was bound to a cross where he preached to those that persecuted him. He preached until he was so exhausted and starving, he died. But he preached Christ with his last breath. Thomas the Doubter was a doubter no longer. They took a lance and ran it through is body. Jude was shot with an arrow. Mathias was stoned and then, because there was still a flicker of life in his body, they cut off his head. Paul, after all his tortures, was beheaded in Rome.

One person of all the early apostles and writers of the New Testament epistles did not die a martyr's death. His name was John. Do you know what happened to him? They dipped him in a vat of boiling oil, and when they brought him out, he still lived! His flesh was so marred, they said he was the ugliest man that ever lived. They banned him to an island called Patmos because they never wanted to see him again. There on that island God gave him the vision--the Revelation of Jesus Christ!

After Christ has called Matthew, Mark, Luke, John,

Peter, and the others, He is going to say unto us, one by one, "What have you done for Me?" Somehow we'll have to stand in front of Him and say, "Oh, I lived in America, and it was so hard to live for You!" I think there will be a hush as people from all the ages realize that if there was anyone who should have been looking for Christ to come, it was us, those who lived in America. If there is anyone who should have the privilege of bringing the gospel to people, it is us! What would it take for God to convince us that we should live for eternity and not for time? Do you love His appearing? Are you ready if Christ were to come?

Will you be at the Judgment Seat of Christ? Have you received Christ in this day and age of grace while there is still time? Will you be among those who sing worship and praise unto His holy name? Will you be there?

Christ Could Come

There is a story about a meeting that took place in hell. Satan gathered his demons and asked them, "What can we do to prevent the message of the gospel from going forth: what shall we tell people?" One worker raised his hand and said, "I will go up and tell them that there never was a Christ." The devil shouted at him, "You've got to be crazy! There's more historical evidence of Christ than of Herod!" Another worker said, "I will tell them the Bible is a lie!" Satan responded, "That's stupid! Look at all the prophecies already fulfilled. They will know it is not a lie!" Another worker said, "I will tell them there was no resurrection." But Satan said, "Then why did Christ's disciples change the way they lived?" The meeting got very quiet. Finally, one of them said, "All right, I have a plan! I will tell them there really is a Bible, and it's true! I will tell them there really is a Christ, and He's powerful! I will tell them there really was a resurrection, and it was no hoax! And

I will tell them that Christ is coming again; He really is coming! But I will tell them this: don't worry about it until tomorrow!" And Satan exclaimed, "THAT'S THE PLAN! That will be our plan to deceive people!"

The PLAN is working! The church of God is deceived and seems to believe the coming of Christ may occur sometime, but not today. If nothing else, I hope and pray that through reading this book, you have become convinced that Christ could come today, even at this very moment. I pray that your life will be changed and that your love for His appearing will grow.

The prophecies have been fulfilled. The stage is set for His return. Every step has been taken, every move has been made. Israel has moved into her role as a sovereign nation of strength and energy (oil) potential. Russia has come forth from its weakness into a position of world power and an ally of nations. The throne of David is set, and the ashes of the red heifer are being sought. The energy crisis threatens even as great advances are being made in technology and travel. We are witnessing the rise to prominence of a final religious New Age movement, the placement of a last political system, and the entry of a final economic condition. Each current event according to Bible prophecy has moved into place according to God's plan.

Are you ready if the next move is the coming of Christ for His bride?